PRAYING
WITH PAUL

For

Ian, Emily and Anna
in grandfatherly affection

Text copyright © Tom Smail 2007
The author asserts the moral right
to be identified as the author of this work

Published by
The Bible Reading Fellowship
First Floor, Elsfield Hall
15–17 Elsfield Way, Oxford OX2 8FG
Website: www.brf.org.uk

ISBN-10: 1 84101 495 8
ISBN-13: 978 1 84101 495 1
First published 2007
10 9 8 7 6 5 4 3 2 1 0
All rights reserved

Acknowledgments
Unless otherwise stated, scripture quotations are taken from The New Revised Standard
Version of the Bible, Anglicized Edition, copyright © 1989, 1995 by the Division of Christian
Education of the National Council of the Churches of Christ in the USA, and are used by
permission. All rights reserved.

Scripture quotations taken from the *Holy Bible, New International Version*, copyright © 1973,
1978, 1984 by International Bible Society, are used by permission of Hodder & Stoughton, a
division of Hodder Headline Ltd. All rights reserved. 'NIV' is a registered trademark of
International Bible Society. UK trademark number 1448790.

A catalogue record for this book is available from the British Library

Printed in Singapore by Craft Print International Ltd

PRAYING
WITH PAUL

TOM SMAIL

PREFACE

The title tells all! I have called the book *Praying with Paul*, rather than *Paul on Prayer*, because its main purpose is not the detailed verse by verse exegesis of Pauline passages but, rather, the exploration of the direction in which these passages point us, so as to shape, correct and enrich our own life of prayer in their light.

Of course, a proper understanding of what Paul writes is still central to such an enterprise, as to see where he is pointing we have first to listen to what he says. Under his guidance we then set out on our journeys into our own relationship with the God who reveals himself to us in Jesus and through the writings of his apostle.

Paul is, as it were, the base camp from which we begin to explore for ourselves all that God has in store for those who pray to him. Paul gives us a trustworthy map of the whole territory and then bids us go and open it up for ourselves. This book is a report of some of the discoveries we make along the way. Paul's name is not on every page, but his teaching is, I hope, the source and the test of all that you will find on these pages.

The book has a long prehistory. Its origin is in a weekend retreat that I led for some of the parishioners of All Saints, Sanderstead, when I was rector there. Since then it has been offered in many different forms to members and leaders, lay and clerical, of many other churches both in this country and overseas. The shape in which it comes now owes a great deal to their expectations, reactions and appreciation.

The Sanderstead connection has persisted in that Mary Duncan, a lay reader in that parish who was present at the initial retreat, has (as with all my recent books) read the draft of the book and offered many helpful suggestions and corrections. Thanks are also due to BRF and Naomi Starkey, their commissioning editor, for their sponsoring of a publication that has, I trust, a sound biblical foundation, but expends most of its space and effort in finding out what building on that foundation might mean for our prayers today.
Tom Smail

✤

CONTENTS

✥

Chapter One

APPROACHING PAUL ON PRAYER

Most of us, when we think of prayer, do not immediately think of Paul and, when we think of Paul, do not immediately think of prayer. For many Christians, prayer has its problems and its failures, but we acknowledge its claim upon us, the challenges with which it confronts us and the intriguing possibilities and promising opportunities it offers.

With Paul it is quite another story. We are more impressed by his incomprehensibility than by his greatness. We latch on to his purple passages like the great hymn to love in 1 Corinthians 13 and read them on all possible occasions, but when it comes to the theological heart of Paul's writings—Galatians, Romans, Colossians—we tend to agree with the writer of 2 Peter when he said of the letters of 'his beloved brother Paul', 'there are some things in them hard to understand, which the ignorant and unstable twist to their own destruction' (2 Peter 3:15–16).

Not wishing to expose our own ignorance or instability, we are very happy to leave Paul's expositions of the mysteries of election and justification to those who are theologically competent while we pass quickly on to more immediate and practical concerns. Add to this the reputation for misogyny that hangs around Paul and it is not hard to see why he often has a bad press even among the churchgoing public and why he will not be the first source to which we turn when we are looking for help with our prayers.

PAUL AND THE PUNDITS

Even sophisticated New Testament theologians differ over how congenial and accessible they find Paul's writings. Archbishop William Temple once recalled a saying of Bishop Lightfoot of Durham, a very eminent 19th-century New Testament scholar, who said that for him the Gospel of John was strange, unfamiliar territory, but he always came back to base and felt at home with Paul. Perhaps it is something about the northern air, sharp in Durham and even sharper north of the border (where I come from), that makes me say the same, and I suppose that is partly why I am trying to persuade you to give Paul a fresh hearing now.

For Temple, however, it was the other way round: John was home territory and Paul a man of jagged peaks and rugged landscapes, so that to explore him was always a challenging and even daunting adventure. As Temple knew, however, it was an adventure well worth embarking on, because of the great if hidden treasure waiting to be discovered among the high rocks and mysterious caves.

GIVE PAUL A CHANCE

For that very reason I am inviting you to explore with me what may be unfamiliar Pauline territory in search of one particular treasure that may until now have been quite hidden, namely his teaching on and his practice of prayer. Like any good guide, I have sussed out the landscape and had a look at the map and can assure any reluctant fellow travellers that the journey will be well worth the effort. In this first chapter we shall look at some of the influences that shape contemporary Christian spirituality in the largely post-Christian West to help us to see how and why what Paul has to tell us about our praying is specially relevant to the problems and difficulties besetting us today. In the following chapters we can then, in closer relationship to particular scriptural passages, fill in the details and draw out the implications of what he is saying to us.

OPPOSITES MEET

Karl Barth and Thomas Merton both died on the same day in 1968, the one from old age in his native Switzerland, the other as the result of an accident with an electric fire during a visit to India, and people have speculated about what these two might have said to each other when they met for the first time at the gates of heaven. Although they were both committed Christians, they were located at opposite ends of the spiritual spectrum. At one end was Barth, the Reformed theologian, standing by common agreement in the very highest rank among the teachers of the Church down all the Christian centuries, the man whose life's work was the production of 15 very fat volumes on the whole range of Christian doctrine. Meeting him from the other end of the spectrum was Merton, the Catholic monastic mystic, also a prolific writer, whose central concern was the exploration of the whole vast area of spirituality and devotion. On the one side was Barth, the careful thinker, the detailed definer and the controversial debater with all the 'i's dotted and all the 't's crossed, the man of the head who could be relentless with opponents and frequently came across as hard, dogmatic and divisive. On the other side was Merton, the man of the heart, more aware of indefinable and transcendent mystery than of revealed truth, finding God more in silence than in speech, more concerned with techniques of devotion than with definitions of doctrine—in danger, at least towards the end of his career, of losing his hold on what is unique about the Christian faith and on the crucial differences of basic faith commitments between his own tradition and that of the Buddhist monks with whom he was in dialogue at the time of his tragic death.

These two, in their different lives and their companionship in their dying, are relevant to us now because they symbolize a divide between theology and spirituality that is a threat and danger to much of Western Christianity today. Certainly in the Anglican circles with which I am most familiar, the proponents of the devotional life have been much closer to Merton than to Barth. For their models and their structures they have often looked more to analytical psychologists than to any theological authority. As a result there has been the constant danger of a disastrous divorce between our thinking and our praying.

Our theology has been in one compartment and our spirituality in another. Theology has been seen to belong to the academic classroom as the specialist province of a professional guild of experts who have skills of scholarship. This puts the whole enterprise beyond the reach not only of most lay Christians but also of many ordained clergy, who, having been subjected to it briefly during their ministerial training, have abandoned it for more immediately relevant pastoral and managerial concerns.

THE TALKERS AND THE SILENT

On the level of ordinary church activities the same potential divide between those who think and those who pray comes out in the contrast between those who frequent the typical parish house group, with its Bible study or its discussion of issues of current Christian concern, and those who prefer a meditation group where the chief ingredient of the gathering is largely unbroken silence. The often highly vocal members of the house group will become silent with embarrassment only when it is suggested that corporate debate might lead on to corporate prayer, whereas the meditators will use their silence to avoid disputable issues of Christian truth and practice that they feel incompetent or afraid to handle. As a result, the lay theologians remain prayerless and the silent pray-ers pay little attention to the theology on which the authentication of what they are doing depends.

PRAYER AND THEOLOGY

In the 1960s and 1970s, as part of a charismatic version of the same anti-theological stance, some people who were rejoicing in a new experience of the Holy Spirit that brought them into a very close and personal relationship to God imagined that they had passed beyond the endless arguments and debates of the theologians into an area of direct and first-hand experience of God with its own sense of certainty and assurance. If you even said the word 'theology' in such circles, you were met with titters and sniggers, the signs of a very unattractive smugness and self-congratulation, hiding a deep nervousness within.

With the second generation of charismatic leaders, the situation has greatly improved in this regard. Untested spiritual experience runs into excess and exaggeration in all kinds of ways, as experienced charismatics and Pentecostals well know; for Christians the test of whether or not our experience has its source in the Holy Spirit is to measure it by the given scriptural gospel, which is the business of any decent theology to expound and explore.

I can remember how during my own charismatic honeymoon in the mid-1960s, when theological reflection was not at the top of my agenda, a wise old Pentecostal minister counselled me, 'Hold on to all your good theology. You are going to need it more than ever now.' How right he has proved to be!

THE PERILS OF PRAYERLESS THEOLOGY

This revolt against theology was to a large extent due to the kind of theology that has sometimes been on offer. That was certainly the case in the charismatic revolt we have been describing, where the prevailing theology that was rejected was often dominated by a 'hermeneutic of suspicion': the authenticity of scripture and the basic affirmations of Christian orthodoxy were either attacked or so modified that they were incapable of sustaining a living relationship with a living God.

I think for example of a sermon by Paul Tillich, one of the theological gurus of the time, in his book *The Shaking of the Foundations*.[1] In the sermon, he expounds Psalm 139 in such a way that the intensely interpersonal relationship with a living and active God, which informs the scriptural text, is explained away in terms of a completely impersonal relationship with an inert and lifeless ground of being or ultimate reality that totally lacks the outgoing love and concern of the God of the Bible. This therefore undermines the personal relationship that makes Christian prayer possible. The same loss of living relationship with a personal God was the chief defect of John Robinson's *Honest to God*,[2] which popularized Tillich and was highly influential in the 1960s in England. No wonder the charismatics wanted none of it!

More generally, the perennial danger of academic theology is that God can become just a subject for endless debate, a debate that undermines our approach to him as the source of our faith and the object of our worship and adoration. The late Colin Gunton used to say that he could always spot a theologian who had stopped preaching, and we could add that it is equally possible to spot a theologian who has stopped praying, if the understanding of God presented by such a person's theology will be one in which prayer is inhibited or indeed excluded.

THEOLOGY NEEDS SPIRITUALITY

It is of course true that any theology worthy of the name has to be academically rigorous and unflinching in its dealings with the doubts and difficulties that always assail Christian faith and never more so than in our own day. In a culture where the gospel is under constant attack from rival religious systems and an influential sceptical secularity, Christian theology has to assert its claims to truth in debate with them.

The only theology able to do that with any degree of credibility will be one that is an expression of the faith it is expounding and defending, that does not stand outside the Christian circle looking in from some mythical position of superior neutrality but stands inside this circle looking out, in order to proclaim a truth that will make sense *of* and perhaps sometimes even *to* the unbelieving world that faith seeks to address. It will, to use the language of Augustine and Anselm, be faith seeking understanding rather than some modern or postmodern understanding wondering about faith. Such a theology will have a creedal 'I believe' at the head and at the heart of it, and the object of that belief will be the living God to whom the scriptures witness.

Because that is so, it will be a theology that not only satisfies the mind but also warms the heart. Good theology will always be both proclamatory and praiseful—both in fact highly characteristic of Barth's own theology. In other words, when you have grasped it, you will be motivated to proclaim the gospel on which it is based; when the wonder of what God has done for the world in Christ comes home to you in its teaching, you will want to fall on your knees in his praise and invoke that mercy upon the world and on yourself in your prayer. It was this kind of theology that set Charles Wesley singing, and one of the earliest expressions of this theology is, as we shall see, the letters of Paul. Far from being an alternative or threat to prayer, it offers a structure for prayer to prosper and grow.

UNTHEOLOGICAL SPIRITUALITY

There is another side to the coin: if theology needs to start with faith and end in prayer, spirituality needs to be grounded in the sort of proclamatory and praiseful theology we have just been describing. When that grounding is ignored and neglected and the prayer of the Church pursued in even relative isolation from the creed of the Church, the resulting compartmentalism can indeed be dire. Decline is guaranteed all the way to pious people indulging in childish gimmicks in an attempt to find God!

Theology—meaning here not so much an academic discipline as

a basic understanding about the nature, character, promises and requirements of the God to whom we seek to relate and respond— is by definition constitutive of any act of prayer. How you pray is entirely dependent on your ideas about the God to whom you are addressing your prayers. The more you know about God, the more you will know what you can expect from God. If you do not know who God is, you will not know what to say to him. An unknown God will inspire only an empty silence and ultimately a despairing prayerlessness.

It is good liturgical order when the reading of the word, its exposition in the sermon and its public articulation in the creed go before the prayers of intercession as the context that makes these prayers possible and meaningful. It also makes sense if those prayers precede the sacrament of Holy Communion in which we engage further with the God of the incarnation, the cross and the resurrection of Jesus Christ.

So also in personal and private prayer, giving attention to God's word through the reading of the Bible provides the proper context for the prayers in which we respond to what God is saying to us. As we shall see in greater depth when we turn to Paul later, our listening will condition our asking at every point. There are some desires deep within us that it is impossible to present to the God of holy love who reveals himself in the gospel except in the form of confession and repentance; other desires so accord with his nature and character that we can offer them to him in expectant confidence that in his own time and way he will fulfil them for us. All the way through, our praying will be shaped by our believing, our asking by our knowledge of the one to whom our requests are directed.

WORD AND SILENCE

It is especially important to understand this when, as in the meditation groups already mentioned, the chief ingredient of prayer is silence. There are, in fact, many different kinds of silence and one of the ways of distinguishing them is to ask how the silence of prayer is related to the speaking of the word.

The idea exists in some contemporary circles that the prayer of silent meditation is in some way superior to the prayer of verbal penitence, intercession and praise, and so speaking and silence are presented as somehow in opposition to each other. Such a divorce is in fact very destructive. A silence that excludes or banishes the words from and about God that form the substance of the Christian faith will be an empty silence, and spiritual vacuums, like physical ones, never remain empty for long. If we are no longer using the silence to listen and speak to the God of the gospel, we can find ourselves listening and speaking to other voices with very different messages or even abandoning a two-sided dialogue with God in favour of an internal monologue in which we are listening and speaking to ourselves.

A silence that is empty of God's word and so open to all sorts of voices from alien sources outside us or self-originated voices inside us is quite different from the rich silence that is informed by the word of God and uses its quietness to contemplate this word in all its depth—indeed to use the word to relate to the mystery of God who has spoken it. His being and love are far beyond what any word can define or contain and it is in such a silence that we can use the knowledge of God given to us by his word to come face to face with the love that surpasses knowledge. That is in fact what Paul prays for the church in Ephesus, that 'you may... know the love of Christ that surpasses knowledge, so that you may be filled with all the fullness of God' (Ephesians 3:19).

The true, faithful and God-given knowledge that comes from God's word can lead us, in the very presence of the God who is beyond all the knowing that words can express, into a contemplation of his presence and a reception of his fullness that is beyond the power of any words to encapsulate; it can only be received in an adoring silence of wordless prayer.

The same thing happens in Paul's letter to the Romans, where, after three chapters of close and often agonized theological argument about God's purposes in Christ for Jews and Gentiles, he throws up his hands and abandons the argument in a kind of adoring despair, which he has reached only by pursuing the argument into a realm of mystery where it could go no further: 'O the depth of the riches and wisdom and knowledge of God! How unsearchable are his judgments and how inscrutable his ways! For who has known the mind of the Lord? Or who has been his counsellor?' (Romans 11:33–34).

It is in the paradoxical relationship between word and silence that Christian prayer finds its distinctive depth and fecundity: the silence arises from the contemplation of the word and the word, in leading us to God himself, ushers us into the pregnant silence of his presence and the mystery of his surpassing grace.

Laurence Freeman makes the point memorably in an article in *The Tablet*,[3] writing out of a long experience of Christian meditation, 'It is a relief to drop the words and gestures, but one appreciates them more for their being drowned in silence... This silence gives language a fallow time, allowing it to be reborn from the eternal youth of the Word: the same old story longing to be known.' It is in that mutual interaction of word and silence and not in the espousal of the one and the exclusion of the other that Christian prayer has its depth and its flourishing.

HELP FROM PAUL

This false dichotomy of word and silence is, as we have seen, only one expression of the even deeper divide between theology and spirituality, between thinking and praying, that characterizes so much contemporary Christianity, at least in the West. We can now go on to see how Paul's approach to prayer is highly relevant to our situation precisely because he insists on holding together what we tend to separate. Before we immerse ourselves in the details of specific Pauline passages in the next chapters, we shall indicate three central features of his theology of prayer which directly confront and correct the dualism that threatens us.

PRAYER IS THEOLOGICAL

Prayer is *theological* in a sense that has been implied but not yet explored in what we have said so far. Statements about God in the Bible and in the classical Christian theology rooted in the Bible claim to represent not just the opinions of their authors but, rather, an objective reality with a life of its own, apart from the thinking of those who speak about it. What the Christian Church says about God claims to have at its heart not our theories and speculations about him but what he has told us about himself in the story of his dealings with his people in the Bible, supremely and definitively in the incarnation, life, death and resurrection of Jesus Christ.

Of course the theology of the Church, like every other human enterprise, is both fallible and imperfect and has been subject to all kinds of distortions and inadequacies, but it lives or dies by its claim that Jesus Christ is the truth, the trustworthy and reliable revelation of ultimate reality, so that in so far as we are faithful to him, we are speaking the truth about God given to us by God himself. The conviction that the gospel he proclaims is not a speculative human theory but an authentic divine revelation is the driving force of the whole of Paul's mission. He is not recommending an inner journey into the ultimate reality at the heart of our own being, but an outward journey in which our attention is not turned in on ourselves but, rather, away from ourselves to events that are outside our competence and control, namely what God has done in Israel and in Jesus.

In these events in outer history there is hidden a true disclosure of the nature of ultimate reality and of its purposes with us and for us. To know God as he is, we have to open ourselves up to it and to that revelation and receive what it is telling us. When we do that, what we know is the truth that we have to maintain and defend.

IN SPIRIT AND IN TRUTH

That is what lies behind the first two chapters of 1 Corinthians, in which Paul presents his gospel of the crucified Christ, which is incomprehensible and unacceptable both to Greek philosophy and its ideas about wisdom and to Jewish religion and its ideas about power: 'But we speak God's wisdom, secret and hidden, which God decreed before the ages for our glory... But, as it is written, "What no eye has seen, nor ear heard, nor the human heart conceived, what God has prepared for those who love him"—these things God has revealed to us through the Spirit; for the Spirit searches everything, even the depths of God' (1 Corinthians 2:7–10).

Through the Spirit, who comes to us from God, we are given access to the truth about the ultimate reality of God, something we could not have reached on our own but which has been made accessible to us through what God has done in Jesus.

Just because the gospel claims to be true, it has about it the exclusiveness of every claim to truth. If a statement is true, then any other statement that contradicts it is by definition untrue, so that if we make a claim for the ultimate truth as it is revealed in Christ, we inevitably question all other claims to religious truth that contradict the gospel, and we have to seek to validate our gospel against them.

It is this truth claim that has made the gospel controversial since it was first enunciated by Paul and the other New Testament writers and that makes it even more controversial in our own postmodern culture where all claims to ultimate truth, especially religious ones, meet with sceptical suspicion and unbelief. All of this has implications for our evangelism and our dialogue with other religions that we cannot pursue now.

TRUTH AND PRAYER

It also has implications for our life of prayer, which, just at this point, leans heavily on our theology but at the same time is able to bring to it reinforcements and confirmations of its own. Our prayer life depends on the validity of the truth of our theology because, when we pray, we need to know that the God to whom we are relating is not a figment of our pious imagination but a reality out there independent of us, who has a life that infinitely transcends us and a life, a will and a purpose of his own that enables him to respond to us.

At the same time our prayer life resources our theology and the truth claims it makes, because it brings us into a relationship with God that is self-authenticating. Through the witness and work of the Holy Spirit to which Paul was referring in the passage we quoted, we are brought into touch with a reality other than and beyond ourselves; yet one that is not only open to us but is making its own gracious initiatives and approaches to us. It is in fact out of this self-authenticating relationship that we are given the conviction of the truth and reality of the gospel expressed by our theology.

Under the influence of the postmodern scepticism surrounding us there have been minority attempts within the Christian community to argue that the gospel might be devotionally helpful without being theologically true. Contemplation of the Christian story could be spiritually purifying and morally inspiring, even if that story was a myth that never happened and if the doctrinal claims built on that story, including its basic affirmation of the existence of God, had been exploded and shown to be unsustainable and unnecessary to our understanding of reality. The story of Jesus could help us to love one another even if it was clear that there was no God to love us. It could help us to liberate our true selves even if there was no divine Saviour to come and save us from ourselves. Anybody who has any experience of the reality of Christian prayer will very quickly see the impossibility of such a position. To be told that we can go on praying when we know that there is nobody or nothing out there to pray to is to cut the throat of the devotional life, not allowing it to breathe or speak any more. It is to try to extract a positive from a negative, something sound and good from something we know to be false and deceptive.

The only credible reason for praying lies in a theology with the affirmation at its heart that there is a living God who can hear and respond to what we say to him. If the theology is tentative, the prayer will be tentative also—'O God, if there is a God, help me now', is more a cry of desperation than of faith, and the person who makes that cry knows that everything depends on whether or not there is any God to answer it. That such desperate cries are actually answered is a witness to the fact that there is such a God and that the measure of his grace towards us far exceeds the measure of our faith towards him.

UNBELIEVING WORSHIP

Even short of this extreme of denying God's existence in our theological thinking and still trying to affirm the validity of our prayer, it is still possible to undermine our worship by a theology that is in blatant contradiction to it. If our thinking is basically an expression of our doubts, it will be hard for our spirituality to be an expression of our faith.

I remember attending a eucharistic service in an Episcopal church in the United States that was liturgically correct and theologically orthodox; assuming that you believed what was being said, you could be greatly helped by it. Afterwards, however, I went to brunch with the people who had been leading the service. In the informal conversation taking place around the table, it soon became clear that they did not believe personally what they had just been proclaiming liturgically. The leaders valued the Bible, creed and sacrament because they made people feel forgiven, affirmed and edified in their spirit, not because they stemmed from and reflected faithfully what God had revealed in Christ; these things were valued because they helped people practically, not because they were ultimately true.

This position reminds me of a man who tries to ride the sea with each foot in a different boat. The courses of the two boats are rapidly diverging to the point where his legs can no longer span the ever-increasing gap between them, so that he is dragged out of both of them and plunged into chaotic waters to drown.

However congenial all this may be to postmodern culture, it is totally destructive of the integrity of the Christian gospel and of those who are lured into a devotional schizophrenia by trying to think one way and pray another way. The inevitable outcome is that the scepticism in the theology will result in paralysis in the prayer. Like Barth and Merton, the man who thinks and the man who prays will both have to go into heaven together or they will not go in at all.

PAULINE INTEGRATION

All of this brings us back to Paul, because in him we find an integration of his thinking and his personal dealings with God, an integration that can help us to identify and heal the disintegration we have been describing.

There is lots of new thinking in Paul; his thinking is one of the great creative influences on the whole Christian tradition from his day to our own. He had the kind of mind that could, in his own words, know the length and the breadth, the depth and the height of what God has done for the world in Christ (see Ephesians 3:18–19). He grasped the implications for the world, the Church and the human person of the way God had fulfilled his covenant with Israel in the coming, living, dying and rising of his Son. It is a thinking that has again and again proved its power to reform, refresh and redirect the life of the Church across the world and down the Christian centuries. But it is never dry thinking; it is undertaken in a context of burgeoning new life, of missionary enthusiasm and personal commitment expressed and confirmed at every point. It does not weigh probabilities but proclaims certainties, because it is a thinking that arises out of and is sustained by the first-hand encounter with the living Christ that began for Paul on the road to Damascus and has been continued and deepened in the life of prayer ever since. The thinking and the praying are so closely interwoven that the one could not be what it is if it were to be disconnected from the other.

To keep company with Paul when he is thinking and praying is to find a prophylactic against the separation imposed upon us by our cultural situation. It is to be called back to that integrated relationship with God in which, in relating corporately and personally to him, we at the same time grasp and are grasped by the truth on which our relating depends. It is that basis in truth and reality that our theology affirms and our prayer expresses.

PRAYER IS DIALOGICAL

If Paul's approach to prayer is theological, in the sense we have been identifying, it is as a consequence *dialogical*. In other words, the theology he inherited from Old Testament Israel, which was affirmed and intensified in Christ, understood prayer as an interaction between two distinct parties: on the one hand a sovereign Creator whose being was constituted by his freedom and his love and, on the other hand, human creatures made in the image of the Creator and so constituted that they could relate to their God in a freedom and love reflecting his own. The history of Israel is seen in terms of a covenant made by a personal God who in his freedom commits himself in faithful love to this people and summons them in their human freedom to respond to him. The essence of that covenant is defined again and again in the Old Testament: 'I will be your God and you shall be my people' (Leviticus 26:12, Ezekiel

36:28). A divine initiative requires and prompts a corporate and individual human response, and it is within the covenant relation of these two personal realities, God and nation, that prayer becomes possible. We *can* pray because God has committed himself to us and so will hear our prayers; we *must* pray because all the concerns of our life have to be pursued within that covenant relationship and so have to be open and offered to God.

All of this is presupposed in the exhortation that Paul makes to the church in Philippi when he tells them that 'the Lord is near. Do not worry about anything but *in everything by prayer and supplication with thanksgiving let your requests be made known to God*' (Philippians 4:5–6). We shall be looking at this whole passage in more detail later on, but for the moment it is enough to note its personal tone, which implies a covenantal relationship between an approachable God and his people, who are invited to bring all their concerns to him in prayer rather than hugging them to themselves in worry, and who await his response to that prayer in expectation and hope. Prayer, in other words, is an ongoing dialogue between God and his people that presupposes their freedom to ask and his freedom to answer. To those of us who have been nurtured in a biblical framework, this approach to prayer is so obvious that it hardly needs explaining. But in our day it very much does need explaining, because it is constantly being challenged and watered down by contemporary ideas about spirituality that can seep into our minds without our noticing at once how different they are from the biblical notion of covenant that we have inherited from the Bible.

MONOLOGICAL SPIRITUALITY

Put it like this: prayer is unambiguously dialogical, whereas much of what is said about spirituality nowadays is inherently monological. In other words, to pray means to make a journey out of and away from ourselves to a God who has a being, a will and purpose far beyond us, and to seek his help.

Spirituality, on the other hand, can be and often is taken to mean a human attribute that is not defined by a relationship with anything or anybody outside ourselves but consists of an exploration of the instinctive and mysterious depths of our own human being, discovered and stimulated by our life experiences and the devotional techniques we employ. This sort of spirituality is indeed a journey into ourselves on the presupposition that the divine is simply the depth of the human and that its resources are available to us in the inner mystery of our own being. Prayer, however, is dialogical because it needs a God to pray to; meditation outside a Judeo-Christian theological framework can become a monologue in which, in the end, we are speaking only to ourselves. There is a massive and profound difference between a divine that is an essential dimension of our own being and a personal God who calls us to go out from ourselves to him. This God promises that from him to us there will come his own Holy Spirit, who will do in us what we cannot do for ourselves and give us gifts and graces that we cannot give ourselves.

For Paul, the depth of our own being apart from God, far from being divine, is the place of our need, our weakness and our misery; help and salvation come not from that place but from the Lord to everybody who calls on his name. If we sit, as we are going to do, in Paul's school of prayer, we shall learn not the techniques of self-exploration or self-fulfilment, but how to relate outside ourselves to the Lord Jesus Christ from whose hands we can seek and receive his Spirit, who can transform us and make us new.

The dialogical nature of Christian prayer is of great importance practically and existentially in the very act of our praying. In my daily intercessions I am constantly under pressure to mull over the perplexities and problems of the people and situations I am praying about and because I can often not understand them and certainly lack any competence to cope with them, the end result of the whole enterprise can be worry and distress.

That is exactly the situation Paul is addressing in the verse from Philippians that we have already quoted: 'The Lord is near. Do not worry about anything but… let your requests be made known to God' (4:5–6). There comes a moment in every time of meaningful intercession when I have to remind myself that the whole point of the exercise is to get what is worrying me off my chest and give it into hands other than mine, the gracious and strong hands of the living God, so that from that moment and until he gives it back to me, it becomes *his* responsibility rather than my own.

Sometimes this can be done in a felt awareness of his presence, sometimes in a lack of any apprehension of presence, in simple faith that he is there and is listening. The doctrinal expression of such a faith is the dialogical and covenantal understanding of God that we have been expounding. Without it, Christian prayer cannot be itself.

PRAYER IS DOXOLOGICAL

Paul's theology of prayer is fundamentally *doxological*, a way of thinking about the God of the gospel that cannot help bursting into praise. We may indeed say that praise and intercession are the twin pillars upon which the life of prayer rests, provided we see the prayer of confession and penitence as a particular kind of intercession in which we ask God in his mercy to restore our relationship with him, a relationship that has been clouded and frustrated by sin.

A glance at the beginning of all the Pauline letters shows that Paul's prayer for his churches is fundamentally one of combined thanksgiving and intercession. Both stem from the grace of God in Christ, whose generosity in the past provokes praise and whose promised generosity in the future gives intercession confidence. The opening verses of Philippians are typical: 'I thank my God every time I remember you, constantly praying with joy in every one of my prayers for all of you… And this is my prayer, that your love may overflow more and more with knowledge and full insight to help you to determine what is best...' (Philippians 1:3–4, 9–10, compare 1 Corinthians 1:4–8, Ephesians 1:15–19).

More generally, when Paul is in thinking mode, so to speak, he talks about 'God', but when his thoughts take wing and turn into joyful acclamations of praise, as they often do, he speaks not of 'God' but of 'Father' or, more specifically, of 'the God and Father of our Lord Jesus Christ'. The point is that 'Father' is a relational word. You can talk *about* God, but you must talk *to* the Father, and Paul keeps going from the one to the other, because his objective thinking about God and his personal relationship to his heavenly Father are built into each other.

It is good to read through the first chapter of Ephesians from this perspective. From its third verse the chapter takes the form of a *berakah*, a formal blessing that Paul would know from the Hebrew liturgies in which he had been reared: 'Blessed be the God and Father of our Lord Jesus Christ...' (1:3). This *berakah* starts with the exclamation of praise and is punctuated by continual outbursts of praise, so that all that he says is 'to the praise of his glory' (1:6, 12, 14). At the same time it contains some highly innovative theological teaching about divine election and that is what prompts the praise. The same *berakah* form with its combination of thinking and blessing is used in the opening verses of 2 Corinthians (1:3ff.)

Such passages are typical of Paul's combination of a rigorous and daring thinking through of the gospel and the prayer that is, both in its intercession and thanksgiving, a doxology of praise. They are together all the way, Barth and Merton, revealed truth and ultimate mystery, the word and the silence, the thinking head and the worshipping heart.

RECLAIMING THE INTEGRATION

The integration offered by Paul could not be more relevant to the spiritual schizophrenia that threatens to disrupt our relationships with God today. It is of course true that, in the differentiation of our personalities and in the distribution of the Spirit's gifts in the body of Christ, some of us will take more easily to the thinking and others to the praying; some of us will latch on to the truth questions and work away at them for a whole lifetime; others will be more on our knees than at our books and will engage in the disciplines and silences of the life of devotion. That is as it should be and each group can immensely enrich the other.

The trouble comes when, in the rush and practicalities of modern living, Christians stop thinking and stop praying, with all the superficiality and deprivation that involves. This book will be of value if it helps even a little to call us back to the hard thinking and praying required by a mature relationship with God.

Those who think need to pray and those who pray need to think if our discipleship is not to go out of shape and become lopsided. Before we go on to the next chapter, it would be good to think about the issues that have been central to this one, very specifically in relation to our churches and ourselves as members of them. Is the balance right between cerebration and celebration, between burrowing for the truth and glorying in the gospel, between measuring the message and meditating on the mystery, between working for God and relying on God? If that balance could be better, what steps need to be taken corporately and personally to make it so?

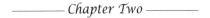

——— *Chapter Two* ———

PAUL AND THE PROBLEMS OF PRAYER

Key Passages: 2 Corinthians 12:7b-10; Romans 8:14-34

If you read only Ephesians, you might think that the heading above was very badly chosen and that for Paul prayer had no problems at all. In Ephesians 1, as we have seen, he is caught up in a rapturous hymn of praise for all that God has done in Christ and when he shares with us his prayers for the church in Ephesus in chapter 3, they are marked by a soaring expectation in the same God 'who by the power at work within us is able to accomplish abundantly far more than all we can ask or imagine' (Ephesians 3:20). This seems to suggest that the life of prayer was for Paul invariably free-flowing, sure-footed and satisfying, carried along by an untroubled confidence in the gospel as a take-off point from which he could soar into unbounded hopefulness and praise.

THE UPS AND DOWNS OF PRAYER

Your instinctive reaction to that, if it is anything like mine, might well be, 'That is great for him, but it is certainly not like that for me.' For many of us and for much of the time prayer is the area of some of our hardest struggles and greatest failures and leaves us feeling guilty and inadequate. When you are feeling like that, there is nothing so depressing as to be confronted with the seemingly effortless triumphs of other people such as Paul in the same area; it puts a great gulf between you and them and erodes your confidence in their ability to help you. What could a man who prays like that know about the difficulties that beset somebody like me who finds it quite hard to pray at all?

For most of us the picture will not be quite as unrelievedly gloomy as just suggested. There will have been days for us, too, when prayer was easy because for a time we were standing on one of those great spiritual mountain tops where God's presence is manifest and almost tangible. At those times, the doubts and questions fall away before the great reality of his coming to us in a fresh discovery of the gospel, in a renewing visitation of the Spirit, in a dramatic deliverance from sin or suffering in which the threatening darkness is unexpectedly turned into the brightening dawn of a new day.

PAUL'S SITUATION AND OURS

These high days probably came more often for Paul than they do for us, not just because he was a bigger and better man, but because he lived in that first glorious springtime of the gospel when everything was fresh and new and flourishing. In the words of Wordsworth, 'Bliss was it in that dawn to be alive, but to be young was very heaven!' (*The French Revolution*, 1804). The Lord was risen, the Church was vibrant, the gospel was glorious; the Lord's hand was at work all around, the tides of hope and expectation were running high and the prayer life of Christians was buoyant in their flow.

There are indeed moments of personal and corporate revival and renewal for us also and many of us would have found it hard to keep going without the refreshment they bring, but they are fewer and less intense in the 21st century than they were in the first, not just because of our personal and ecclesiastical defects, but because our whole context and situation are very different.

What was new then has become old and familiar now; what was

clear then has become ambiguous now because of all the debate that has analysed it and all the doubt that has been cast upon it. What was growing in Paul's lifetime has been in long decline as far as the once Christian West is concerned, and our prayers that this decline should be reversed have until now remained unanswered. All the many prophecies of revival have remained unfulfilled and often seem to have their source in the dreams of the despairing rather than in the promises of the Lord.

Paul lived in the glow of the first Pentecost whereas we have had to live through the dull days of a spiritual winter, praying for a new Pentecost, which has often seemed to be starting but has not yet arrived. All this means that the feel of prayer is much more upbeat for someone in Paul's position than it is for someone in ours; the resurrection spirituality of Ephesians comes more easily to him than to us.

PRAYER AND THE CROSS

There is, however, another side to all this that can bridge the seemingly wide gap between Paul and us. Not just in Paul's theology but also in Paul's experience, the resurrection is never without the cross; the glory of the one is made possible by and finds its meaning in the suffering of the other. When Paul is reviewing his ambitions for the future in Philippians, he says that he wants to share in both the agony and the victory of Jesus: 'I want to know Christ and the power of his resurrection and the sharing of his suffering by becoming like him in his death, if somehow I may attain the resurrection from the dead' (Philippians 3:10–11). Such a spirituality embraces not only triumph but also failure, not only the revealed glory of a manifestly present God but days when that God appears to have turned away his face and dire and deadly things have their way with us as they did with Jesus on the cross.

If Ephesians and its boundless expectations lie at one end of the Pauline spectrum, 2 Corinthians with its picture of an apostle beset with difficulties and threatened by abandonment lies at the other: 'We are afflicted in every way, but not crushed; perplexed, but not driven to despair; persecuted, but not forsaken; struck down, but not destroyed; always carrying in the body the death of Jesus, so that the life of Jesus may also be made visible in our bodies' (2 Corinthians 4:8–10). That sounds like a Christian experience more akin to our own, hoping for the power of the resurrection to manifest itself amidst a life burdened by the failure and perplexity of the cross.

PAUL'S REFUSED REQUEST

It is in this same letter that Paul tells us how the interplay of cross and resurrection has actually worked out in his life of prayer. In chapter 12 he starts off from the mystical experiences in which he was 'caught up into the third heaven... and heard things that are not to be told, that no mortal is permitted to repeat' (vv. 2, 4)—a wonderful entry into the new world of the resurrection if ever there was one. In this very context, however, Paul tells us about a prayer request that was not granted, precisely because in the full glow of that resurrection experience he had to be reminded that he was still a man who lived under the cross: 'Therefore to keep me from being too elated, a thorn was given me in the flesh, a messenger of Satan to torment me, to keep me from being too elated' (v. 7).

Down the years commentators on this passage have famously speculated about the nature of Paul's thorn in the flesh and suggestions, supported by ingenious arguments, have ranged from bad eyesight through attacks of epilepsy to persecution by Jews, with no firm conclusion likely to be reached. Perhaps Paul tells us all that we need to know when he says that it was sore and it was satanic. It was something that caused him continual torment and that he saw as a device of the powers of evil to undermine his ministry and in that way to frustrate the saving purposes of God.

For both these reasons Paul wanted rid of it and in prayer asked God to set him free from it: 'Three times I appealed to the Lord about this, that it would leave me' (v. 8). He had learned the lesson of the parables of Jesus in Luke 12 that prayer often requires persistence if it is to prevail; so he prayed to God not once but three times that this impediment might be taken from him. Presumably in his praying about his disability (whatever it was), Paul asked three times because on the first two askings he received no answer. Indeed, this underlines one of the central problems that we all encounter, namely, what do we do when we ask and in reply God says nothing at all? On the third asking, the answer did come, but it was not the one that was sought or expected. It was right and understandable that Paul should seek God's help in being relieved of something that, by absorbing his energies, was impeding his ministry; when we suffer we are right to come to God to get us out of our pain. In the ministry of Jesus many came with such requests and were graciously and positively answered in his gifts of forgiveness, healing and deliverance. But here in Paul, almost uniquely for the New Testament, such a request for healing and deliverance is made and refused: 'He said to me, "My grace is sufficient for you, for my power is made perfect in weakness"' (v. 9).

COPING WITH UNEXPECTED ANSWERS

This raises the question of whether or not we can make sense of a response to our prayers that is, in relation to what we asked, a denial pointing in quite a different direction than the one we wanted to take. There are problems not just about receiving no answer, but even more about receiving an answer that is 'wrong' and not the one we expected or sought. There is a real danger that we can be so set on getting what we wanted and so closed and unsubmissive to God's alternative strategy for meeting our need that we cannot hear what he is saying to us and conclude quite wrongly that he is not saying anything at all.

To put the same thing in a different way, and linking up with something we said in Chapter One, when we pray we encounter a personal God who has a will and a purpose of his own, which some-times coincide with our will and purpose so that what we seek can be given. But at other times, in the freedom of his love, God will choose to fulfil his good purposes for us in ways unwelcome to us. When that happens, it is hard to understand, because it requires us to go on coping with suffering and frustrations that try our patience and press upon us so heavily that we wonder how we can continue to bear them without breaking.

THE PROMISE IN THE REFUSAL

It must have been a very great disappointment to Paul that there was to be no relief from his disability, that the wounding thorn would continue to ache and stress him at every step he took. But, however long it took to get to this point, by the time he came to write this letter he had come to see the promise hidden in the refusal: 'My grace is sufficient for you'—you won't be in this alone; you will not be miraculously delivered but you will be continually supported and con-stantly supplied. At the same time he had come to terms with God's strategy with him: 'My power is made perfect in your weakness'—my purposes with you will be more powerfully enabled when you are in constant dependence on me in your weakness than if you were to be exulting in your own strength. That promise and strategy have in fact worked out in his own subsequent experience so that he can now affirm and embrace them: 'Therefore I am content with weaknesses, insults, hardships, persecutions and calamities for the sake of Christ; for whenever I am weak, then I am strong' (v. 10).

TAKING OUT AND TAKING THROUGH

We have an important clue to how Paul can reach this contentment with his sufferings when he says that it is 'for the sake of Christ'

(v. 10). We have already seen how the gift of deliverance and healing relates to the ministry of Jesus; we can also see how the refusal or at least the deferral of deliverance and healing relates to the cross of Jesus. Jesus' prayer in Gethsemane to have the cup of suffering taken from him was refused just as surely as Paul's prayer over his undefined disability was. From his prayer in one garden to his burial in another, the dire events that brought Jesus to his death continued without any divine relief or intervention. God did nothing for Jesus until people had done their worst to him; the way to his vindicating resurrection on the third day led through the facing of the direst kind of death, not by evading or avoiding it.

It was only in the agonizing weakness of the pain and desolation of Calvary that God's reconciling purpose could be perfectly fulfilled and, as Paul came to see that in relation to his prayer, so Jesus came to see it in his own prayer in Gethsemane when he abandoned his request for rescue and said to his Father, 'If this [cup] cannot pass from me unless I drink it, your will be done' (Matthew 26:42).

There will be times when God in the freedom of his love will take us out of the situations that are troubling and threatening to destroy us; as people came to Jesus in Galilee and sought his help and his healing, so the way stands open for us to come to him today. As help and healing were graciously granted then, they are, when God so pleases, granted now, as many can testify.

But the deepest of God's redeeming works is done not in Galilee but at Calvary, when God does not take his Son *out of* his suffering but *through* it to a different kind of triumph that can be achieved only in this way, where the risen Jesus still has wounds to show in his hands and side, 'rich wounds yet visible above in beauty glorified.'[4]

Because Paul sees his own Christian life as a following of Jesus along the road that led him through Good Friday to Easter— because Paul knows the power of the resurrection through the sharing of the sufferings—he can go on coping with the specific suffering represented by his 'thorn in the flesh', both because he has the promise of Christ's grace to support him and because he can see from the analogy between himself and Jesus that it is in this way only that God's deepest purposes for him can be fulfilled.

This also applies to you and me. As we try to understand what is going on in our prayerful dealings with God and the problems they raise, we have to reckon with the fact that, along with the times when God gives us what we ask and makes us glad and grateful for what he has done for us, there will be other times when the answer we get will not be the answer we want. This is not because his love has turned from us, but because what love wants to do in us and through us can be done only by the patient enduring of suffering. Through what happens in the dark bad hours, the door to the new life of Easter is ultimately opened to us. We have to be ready for the answer to our prayers sometimes to be, '[My] power is made perfect in [your] weakness' (2 Corinthians 12:9) and to believe, when we cannot yet see, that often it is in and through weakness that we can become strongest.

PRAYER WEAKNESS CONFESSED

That word 'weakness' is in fact the connecting link between the passage in 2 Corinthians that we have been thinking about and the other passage in Romans 8 that will occupy us for the rest of this chapter and the whole of the next. The Greek word in both passages is *astheneia*—a strong word meaning sickness, powerlessness, disability and so also weakness. In the passage from 2 Corinthians it applies to Paul's condition when the thorn is pressing on his flesh; in Romans 8:26, it characterizes the problems he experiences specifically in relation to prayer: 'The Spirit helps us in our *astheneia*; for we do not know how to pray as we ought.' In both letters the word *astheneia* is set in a context of positive promise. Paul is assured that when he is weakened by the thorn, he is at that very point open to the power of God, and Paul, as he acknowledges his weakness in prayer, also acknowledges that it is precisely then that the Spirit of God comes to his aid.

Before we turn to the help that the Spirit brings, we need to see that for Paul as well as for us, prayer has its flip side; it is by no means a straightforward and triumphant asking and receiving, but perplexities and anxieties are connected with both. We might say in general that when Paul looks away from himself at the nature and action of the God to whom he prays, he can contemplate receiving responses from God that far exceed all that he can ask or imagine (Ephesians 3:20). When he concentrates on himself, however, and on the nature and character of his own devotional life, it all looks different: he becomes aware that he is not all that good at it. It is full of problems and perplexities that he does not know how to deal with on his own. At this point most of us can make common cause with him; his expectations may far exceed ours, but when he acknowledges that there are problems, we know exactly what he is talking about.

THE PROBLEMS OF PRAYER

The Bible translators and commentators are not quite sure what kinds of problems Paul is identifying in Romans 8:26. It can be validly translated with the New International Version as 'we do not know *what* we ought to pray for', or equally well with the New Revised Standard Version as 'we do not know *how* to pray as we ought.' The former refers to the *content* and the latter to the *manner* of our praying. Both can be problem areas and it could well be that Paul had both in mind; at any rate it will be helpful to look at both a little more closely.

WHAT SHALL I PRAY FOR? THE PROBLEM OF WRONG ASKING

As far as the content of our prayers is concerned, we are often left wondering if we have asked for the right thing in our intercessions for other people. To take an obvious example, when I am praying for somebody who is ill, is it always the way of faith to ask for their recovery? Is there a time when I should be content to ask for them to have the strength and courage to see it through and leave the outcome to the promise of God? Is there even a time when I should be praying for a good and holy dying? Sometimes the one and sometimes the other is appropriate and it can be difficult to know from case to case which is which.

When one of my very dear ministerial colleagues was lying in the terminal stages of ovarian cancer, people from the church, who knew pretty well how things stood with her, nevertheless kept sending her cards to say that they were praying for a full and speedy recovery. Was that great faith or was it simply a faint-hearted failure to come to terms with what was clearly happening? My friend herself did not say anything but simply pointed to the cards on a shelf facing her bed and smiled; she was past all that and prayers set on her healing were at that point a distraction from what she and those closest to her were focusing on—her leaving of one life and her anticipation of another. That was where, for her at that point, the presence and promise of God were most graciously and power-fully found.

Sometimes, as in this case, wrong asking can spring from an inability or an unwillingness to discern what God is doing in a situation. Left to ourselves, such lack of discernment can afflict us all and make it harder to receive what God is actually saying to us in response to our prayers. For some people this is a cause of great anxiety. They have a fear, sometimes on a conscious level, but more often unconsciously under the surface, that if they ask for the wrong thing, their prayer will be invalidated and God will not respond to it. It is good to ask ourselves how much we think asking for the right thing matters. Does God say, 'What a pity; they asked wrongly, so we can't answer' or can he take a misguided and undiscerning request and make it the means by which his real will can be done in the life of the person prayed for?

A fuller answer to these questions will open up as we look at the positive teaching about prayer that Romans 8 contains, but in the meantime we can get some preliminary help by looking back at what we have already discovered about Paul's prayer in 2 Corinthians. The request to have his satanic disability removed was itself a mistaken request, running contrary to the way in which God was going to deal with the situation that had been opened up to him by Paul's prayer, but the very fact that he had prayed for the wrong thing brought Paul in touch with the right answer: 'My grace is sufficient for you' (v. 9).

What matters when we pray about something is not what we ask for, but that we are putting our needy situation into God's hands, thus opening it up to what he wants to say and do about it. Our prayer, whatever its specific content, can then become the means by which his loving purpose can reach down into it. In other words, a wrong prayer can still be an effective prayer because it links up a situation to God and to what he wants to do about it; if our attitude is one not just of asking but of listening, it can be the means by which we hear how God proposes to act, even if his proposal to us may be quite different from our original proposal to him.

HOW SHOULD I ASK? ASKING IN THE WRONG WAY

To turn now to the other possible interpretation of Romans 8:26, more often our sense of inadequacy has to do with problems that arise less from the *content* and more from the *method* of our praying. We ask not so much, 'Did I ask for the wrong thing?' but rather, 'Did I ask for it in the wrong way?'

Was there some unforgiven sin standing between me and God, so that my prayer did not get through? Remembering again what Jesus had to say about the friend who came at midnight and went on knocking until the door was answered (Luke 11:5–8) and the widow who pestered the unjust judge until he gave her the verdict she sought (Luke 18:2–7), did I give up too soon? If I had gone on praying a bit longer, would the desired answer have been given? Or, perhaps most pressing and guilt-engendering of all, was there enough faith in my praying?

Prayer and pardon

The fact that unforgiven sin can indeed invalidate our praying and God's response to it is implicit in Jesus' dealing with the paralysed man in Mark 2:1–12, where the first words he said to the man, 'Son, your sins are forgiven', opened the way to the following, 'I say to you, stand up, take your mat and go to your home.' We need to keep short accounts with God if he is to fulfil all his good purposes for us, but the promise of forgiveness, utterly gracious and totally unlimited, is at the heart of the gospel for our seeking, our believing and our receiving: 'If we confess our sins, he who is faithful and just will forgive us our sins and cleanse us from all unrighteousness' (1 John 1:9). In our prayers we have to engage in confession, seek pardon and submit to cleansing before we seek anything else at all. We should also pay heed to the words of Jesus that effective prayer depends not only on our receiving forgiveness but also on our imparting it: 'Whenever you stand praying, forgive, if you have anything against anyone; so that your Father in heaven may also forgive you your trespasses' (Mark 11:25).

Prayer and persistence

We shall come back to the question of persistence in greater detail later. In a preliminary way we can now put together the insights of the parables of Jesus and the experience of Paul over his 'thorn in the flesh' and say that you go on praying about something until you get an answer—either, as in the parables, the answer you were looking for, or, as with Paul, an answer that you were not looking for but that, as you persist in your prayer, you become able to hear. The more you pray, the more sensitive you become to what God wants to do about whatever you are offering to him. Persistence in prayer is not the same as mere repetition; it is not just saying the same thing over and over again, but it is a waiting in the presence of God until he is ready to speak to you and you are ready to hear what he says.

Prayer and faith

For light on the vexing question about the relationship between prayer and faith we have to look to Jesus rather than Paul, and we can do so here only in summary form because the material in the Gospels is too extensive and many-sided for us to do it anything like full justice here.

It is clear, however, that from start to finish the ministry of Jesus was enabled by the faith he inspired in those who came to him and frustrated when it encountered unbelief, either in those he sought to help or in his own disciples when they undertook to act in his name. It is also clear that faith in God is never easy and by its very nature is open to attack and doubt. Faith is the conviction that God is willing and able to do what we ask and, in Paul's phrase, 'far more than we can ask or imagine' (Ephesians 3:20), even when that seems unlikely and even impossible, because the situation we are facing appears to be quite inflexible and closed to redemption.

Such a conviction is never a serene and unclouded certainty but has always to be found and affirmed against the doubts based on the evidence of hard experience that what faith asks does not often happen. The question therefore arises: how can we come by such faith? What is it that enables us to trust God's promises when our common sense and the sceptical world around us are crying out that they can never be kept?

The truth is that faith is increased by prayer. We do not somehow work ourselves up into a vibrant faith before we start to pray; rather, as we open ourselves to the presence and promises of God in our praying, the reality of his power and love becomes more and more credible to us and the doubts and experiences that challenge him are overcome by our contact with him. I have found again and again that when I take time to expose myself to the presence and promises of the God who speaks to me in his gospel, I become more and more persuaded of his will and ability to offer me help for the people and situations I bring to him. This is perhaps the process Jesus is describing when he says, 'Truly I tell you, if you say to this mountain, "Be taken up and thrown into the sea," and if you do not doubt in your heart, but believe that what you say will come to pass, it will be done for you. So I tell you, whatever you ask for in prayer, believe that you have received and it will be yours' (Mark 11:23–24). I can make sense of these verses if they are seen not as a harsh command to force ourselves into believing impossible things, but as the description of a filtering process that takes place within the act of our praying. Because we are concentrating on God, our initial doubts and the sceptical attitude from which we start no longer dominate the scene, but we become tuned in to God's possibilities of previously unbelievable responses to what we have presented to him. If we look at ourselves and our own faith, it will wither away into nothing, but if we look away from ourselves to God, as we do when we pray, then our faith will go grow and become the channel for his help and healing.

When we look at the story of the healing of the boy with the evil spirit in Mark 9:17–29, we see this process at work. On the one side are the disciples who, in the absence of Jesus, fail to make any impact on the sick boy. Although they had enough faith to try, it collapsed before the unyielding nature of the situation and the scepticism of the crowd, and it was their doubts that prevailed. When later the disciples asked Jesus, '"Why could we not cast it out?" He said to them, "This kind can come out only through prayer"' (Mark 9:28–29). Only people living in close communion with God will be able to believe in the power of God enough to release it into situations that deny and defy it.

On the other side is the father of the boy, who also has his doubts but stands in the presence of Jesus who says to him, 'All things can be done for the one who believes' (v. 23). The father responds by saying with great honesty, 'I believe; help my unbelief!' (v. 24). He confesses his doubts, but in the very confessing of them repudiates them, 'I believe.' When he looks at Jesus, this man who, left to himself, would be a sceptic, becomes a believer. Although his faith may be no bigger than a grain of mustard seed (see Matthew 17:20), yet, because of what he sees in Jesus, he puts himself on the side of his faith, thus opening the way for the impossible to happen and for his son to be made whole. The more we seek Jesus in prayer, the more the grip of doubt can be loosened and the openness of faith realized.

PAUL'S OWN ANSWER

These are perhaps some of the problems of prayer hinted at when Paul says that he does not know how to pray as he ought and we have looked past Paul to Jesus to see how he might help us to deal with them. But Paul also has his own answers to his problems that are deeply dependent upon and consonant with those of Jesus, but are expressed in his own language and his own way. To these we now turn.

PRAYER AND THE HOLY SPIRIT

Here is the signpost that points in the direction Paul wants to take us; at the very point at which he is facing his own perplexity and disability about prayer, Paul starts to speak not about our need for faith and persistence but about the help that comes from the Holy Spirit: 'In the same way, the Spirit helps us in our *astheneia*. We do not know how or what we ought to pray for, but the Spirit himself intercedes for us (Romans 8:26, NIV).

PRAYER AS GOD'S GIFT

It will take the rest of this chapter and all of the next to spell out what this verse means, but the basic point is that authentically Christian prayer starts not with us but with God. It does not originate in our thoughts and desires and then move out from us to make contact with God. On the contrary, the mention of the intercession of the Spirit here underlines the fact that prayer has its source and origin in God: before we offer it to him, he gives it to us. It is the Spirit of God who is the source of our intercession. He comes to us from God, bringing with him into our deep hearts the prayer that we can then make our own and offer back to the God who has given it to us.

What we are saying here has to be seen in the context of the main message of the letter to the Romans. In the earlier chapters, Paul has been making his basic point, over and over again and in many different ways, that, because we are sinners, we cannot attain a right relationship with God by our own efforts to keep his law and obey his commandments. All such efforts at self-justification are doomed to failure. We cannot get into a right relationship with God by relying at all on what we do for him, but rather by relying on what he has done for us in Christ incarnate, crucified and risen. A right relationship with God therefore is a matter not of performance but of reception; it comes to us not as a reward for our own efforts, but as an undeserved gift won for us by God's Son and given for us to receive and enjoy by God's Spirit.

What is said about prayer in Romans 8 is entirely in line with the approach of the whole letter. Because prayer is at the very centre of a right relationship with God, we are here invited to think of prayer not first and foremost as a hard and demanding work to be accomplished but, rather, as a free and gracious gift to be received. Whatever level of theological sophistication we may have reached on the conscious level of our thinking, deep down under the surface in most of us is the idea that prayer and indeed all worship is something that we must do in order to get in touch with God. According to this view, God is far above us up there in heaven in the transcendence of the Creator over his creatures and in the holiness that separates him from sinners; it is our intimidating task to reach him with our worship and win from him a favourable answer to our prayers. He is, as it were, the target nearly beyond our reach and our prayers are the arrows we fit into the bow of our faith in the uncertain hope of hitting a bullseye. If the metaphor is crude, so also is the theology that it expresses!

Prayer as technique

In such circumstances it is of prime importance to have a bow of faith strong enough to span the distance and an aim accurate enough to make a hit. For this way of thinking, everything depends on us and our learning the right techniques to win us success. All those questions about whether we have been asking for the right thing for long enough and with sufficient faith loom large—so large that they turn us in on ourselves and our perplexities and thus distract our attention from God, undermining our confidence in his willingness to hear us and his grace to respond to us.

Some fruitful questions

What if prayer were not this kind of hard task that often daunts us, but a free gift graciously given and to be gratefully received? What if it were not the testing means by which we try to reach God but the kind provision that he makes to reach us? What if the answer to the problems we have been thinking about were not for us to solve by schooling ourselves to pray better, but to turn our attention away from ourselves and our efforts and instead to tune in to the perfect prayer that the Spirit is already praying in our hearts? What if the central clue to the whole life of worship and indeed to all Christian living were what Paul says in Galatians 2:20:

'It is no longer I who live, but it is Christ who lives in me'?

It can be helpful to make this general statement specific in situations that, if we faced them alone, could worry and disturb us, for example: 'It is no longer I who am going into this difficult interview, but Christ who is going in with me.' In the present context this means that when we are getting ready to pray, we should realize that right from the start we are not on our own: 'It is no longer I who am responsible for what is going to happen in this prayer time, but Christ who will be praying in me.' It works: again and again I have approached my own morning prayer time with heaviness and reluctance, and again and again I have discovered the mysterious nature of what is going on there—what I have got out of it has been immeasurably more than what I have put into it; my eyes have been opened, my mood has been changed, my hopes have been raised because of his giving to me in my praying to him. Because Paul approaches prayer in that way, he passes over questions of technique almost in silence. For him the issues about how we are to pray are secondary and can be helpfully addressed only when we have tuned in to the nature and character of the God to whom we pray.

The way you conduct any relationship depends on what sort of person you are relating to and it is no different with God. The kind of relationship we can have with a God who is remote and repelling in his holiness will be quite different from the relationship we can have with a God who is open and outgoing towards us in his redeeming and transforming love. To find out what Paul has to say to us about how we can pray rightly, we have to look at all he says about the God to whom we pray in the whole of Romans 8.

PRAYER AND THE TRINITY

As we do so, we shall see that the relationship with God that, for Paul, makes Christian prayer possible—a relationship expressed by Christian prayer—is much more complex than we might at first have expected. It is in fact a trinitarian relationship. As Gordon Fee puts it, 'In these chapters Paul's trinitarian presuppositions stand out everywhere. God is the prime mover, the principal actor in all things. God has brought about this salvation, this new people for his name, through the death and resurrection of his own Son (8:3). And God has brought all of it to realisation through the gift of his Holy Spirit, who is also the Spirit of his Son.'[5]

Paul did not, of course, have anything like a worked-out doctrine of the Trinity; that came much later. The very nature of the gospel he was exploring, however, led him to the conviction that the God it revealed to us was simultaneously and equally the Father above us, the Son incarnate as one of us and the Holy Spirit working among us and within us. We have only to draw attention to three central verses in Romans 8 to realize that Paul knew perfectly well that the Christian relationship to God was in fact a threefold relationship to a triune God.

In verses 15–17 he speaks of how God the Father is involved in our praying: 'For you did not receive a spirit of slavery to fall back into fear, but you have received a spirit of adoption. When we cry "Abba, Father!" it is that very Spirit bearing witness with our spirit that we are children of God, and if children, then heirs, heirs of God and joint heirs with Christ—if, in fact, we suffer with him so that we may also be glorified with him.' Our relationship to *Abba* is at the centre of all our praying, but it is at the same time a trinitarian relationship because our access to the Father is made possible only through the Son and in the Spirit.

The role of the incarnate, crucified and ascended Son in our praying is, however, the explicit subject of verse 34 of the same chapter, where Paul speaks of 'Christ Jesus who died, yes, who was raised, who is at the right hand of God, *who indeed intercedes for us*.' The incarnate Christ is now at the right hand of God and his work there is a perpetual prayer of intercession on behalf of his people. The implication is that, if this is central to his ministry, it will be central to the ministry of all who belong to him as well.

Alongside there is also a mysterious involvement of God the Holy Spirit in our praying. So verses 26–27, which, as we have seen, speak of our *astheneia* in prayer, also tell of the Holy Spirit's activity deep within our praying to heal our sickness and to remedy our incapacity: '*that very Spirit intercedes with sighs too deep for words*. And God who searches the heart knows what is the mind of the Spirit, *because the Spirit intercedes for the saints according to the will of God*.' The answer to the problems of our praying is the other kind of praying that is simultaneously going on in our hearts and in our midst—the perfect prayer of the Spirit.

Summarizing all this in preparation for our detailed expounding of it in the next chapter, we can already devise something like a trinitarian definition of Christian prayer: the Father is the one *to* whom we pray, the Son is the one *with* whom we pray and the Spirit is the one *in* whom we pray. Because these three are one God and so fulfil their different roles in total union and interdependence, in our praying we have ourselves to take account of the distinctive part that each divine person plays within it and indeed within the whole gospel story, which is the context of all Christian praying.

Prayer to the Father

In our praying, as in the whole revealed gospel, the Father is both the source from which everything else comes and the destination to which everything else returns. It is the Father's love for us that starts it all: 'God so loved the world that he gave his only Son' (John 3:16). In his will for restored relationship with us he sends his Son and his Spirit out from his own life into our life and our world so that they, each in his own distinctive way, may bring us back to him.

Jesus says, 'I am the way, and the truth, and the life. No one comes to the Father except through me' (John 14:6). The Son is uniquely and irreplaceably the way to the Father, but the Father, not the Son, is the destination to which we are called to return.

This is also the rule of our praying: 'Through him [Christ] both of us have access in one Spirit *to the Father*' (Ephesians 2:18). That is exactly what prayer is—access to the Father—and it is at the heart of the distinctive prayer that Jesus gives to his disciples: 'Pray then in this way: "Our Father…"' (Matthew 6:9). That is what Paul is echoing here: 'And by him [the Spirit] we cry "Abba, Father"' (Romans 8:5, NIV).

Prayer with the Son

In our praying, just as in the whole revealed gospel, the Son in his incarnation, without ceasing to be God and sharing equally the deity of the Father, is made man and so stands in complete solidarity with us on the human side of our relationship with the Father, dealing with the Father on our behalf. What Paul says here about the intercession of Christ is consonant with that. He is not the one to whom we pray, but his prayer on our behalf and our identification with it give our intercession its confidence and its validity.

Prayer in the Spirit

Again, in our praying just as in the whole revealed gospel, the Holy Spirit is identified as the one who takes what the Father has done on our behalf through the Son and involves us personally and corporately in it. As Jesus promises in John 16:14: 'He [the Spirit] will take what is mine and declare it to you.'

That is in line with how Paul expounds the work of the Spirit in Romans 8. The cry *Abba*, which is first of all the cry of Jesus, becomes in the Spirit our cry: 'God has sent the Spirit of his Son into our hearts, crying "Abba! Father!"' (Galatians 4:6)—a trinitarian statement if ever there was one. It is the same with our intercession: what the Son prays *for* us at the right hand of the Father (Romans 8:34), the Spirit prays *in* us at the roots of our being and the bottom of our hearts (v. 29).

To summarize, we have seen that Paul's teaching on prayer in this chapter is intimately related to both the doctrine of salvation by grace that dominates this letter and the whole trinitarian structure of the gospel. The problems of prayer are best addressed when we receive it as the gift of the triune God. That is the basic structure of our praying. In the next chapter we shall begin to see how much help that trinitarian structure offers in the daily reality of our praying.

❖

—————— *Chapter Three* ——————

PAUL AND THE
RESOURCES OF PRAYER

Key Passage: Romans 8:14-34

In 1987, the Doctrine Commission of the Church of England published a report, *We Believe in God*,[6] and gave the chapter on the doctrine of the Trinity the striking title 'God as Trinity—an Approach through Prayer'. The main point of this chapter is that the trinitarian understanding of God, which is basic and definitive for orthodox creedal Christianity, has its roots not in metaphysical speculation or remote theological theories accessible only to a guild of elite experts, but rather in the practice and experience of prayer as Paul describes it in this passage. The doctrine has its raison d'être not in the university classroom but in the worshipping congregation. Our knowledge of God as Father, Son and Holy Spirit becomes relevant and practical because, when we worship, it is such a God whom we meet.

To quote the report: 'Usually it dawns bit by bit on the person praying that this activity, which at first sight seems all one's own doing, is actually the activity of another. It is the experience of being "prayed in", the discovery that "we do not know how to pray as we ought" (Romans 8:26), but are graciously caught up in a divine conversation passing back and forth in and through the one who prays "the Spirit bears witness with our spirit" (Romans 8:16). We come to prayer empty-handed, aware of weakness, inarticulacy, and even of a certain hollow "fear and trembling", yet it is precisely in these conditions... that divine dialogue flows.'[7]

This approach is very much in line with what we have said in Chapter 2. To pray and worship is indeed to be caught up into the distinctive interrelational exchanges, the dialogue, or perhaps better 'trialogue' between the Father, the Son and the Holy Spirit, which is the framework first of the gospel story itself and then of the new relationship with God that the gospel makes possible. It is our admission into that divine interrelating that gives us access to the resources that make our prayers acceptable and effective with God. We now go on to explore how it works out in daily detail as we pray *to* the Father, *with* and *through* the Son and *in* the Spirit. To do so, we shall fill out and complement Paul's teaching here by looking at other parts of the New Testament as well.

PRAYING TO THE FATHER

So, what does it mean for our prayers that they are addressed to the God whom Jesus invited us to name as 'Our Father'? For Paul, it is that very name, put on our lips by none other than the Spirit of God himself, that gives us the right to pray and the confidence that our prayers will be heard and answered: 'When we cry "Abba! Father!" it is that very Spirit bearing witness with our spirit that we are children of God, and if children, then heirs, heirs of God and joint heirs with Christ' (Romans 8:15–17).

FATHERHOOD—DIVINE AND HUMAN

The use of the Aramaic word *Abba* by Paul links him with Jesus, because *Abba* was uniquely and unforgettably Jesus' own name for God. Every prayer that he is recorded as praying, with the single exception of the cry of dereliction from the cross, had *Abba* in front of it. For both Mark and for Paul the word was so characteristic of Jesus that it was included without translation in their Greek texts.

What it means for Christians to call God Father has to be

understood in relation to Jesus and not in any other way. The ideas of fatherhood that we have picked up from our own culture or from our relationship with our own earthly fathers do not tell us what kind of father God is. The fact that these earthly fathers may have been patriarchal in their domination of us, indulgent in their attitudes to us or distant in their indifference towards us does not tell us anything at all about the fatherhood of God as it is revealed and defined by Jesus.

Paul makes precisely that point when, as part of his prayer for the Ephesians, he bows his knee 'before the Father, from whom every family in heaven and on earth takes its name' (Ephesians 3:14). In other words, God's fatherhood defines ours and not ours his. We are not to take any notion of fatherhood derived from our own experience, project it upwards on to God and then complain that it is sexist or patriarchal and needs to be either discarded or supplemented by other, more feminist-friendly or politically correct names. For Jesus, and for Paul following Jesus, *Abba* is the name that God has given us to use through his Son, so our first priority is not to criticize or replace it but to understand what Jesus meant by it. He must be allowed to define it for us without its being confused or conflated with these other ideas that we often bring to it. For Paul in particular, the New Testament name of God is not just Father, but, when spelt out formally, the God and Father of our Lord Jesus Christ (compare 2 Corinthians 1:3, Ephesians 1:3). The kind of Father that he will be to us is the kind of Father he has already shown himself to be to Jesus.

Names and people

To put the same thing in another way, it is people who give meaning to names rather than names that give meaning to people. In the church to which we belong, there is a young girl called Meadow. If you take the name by itself, it makes you think of cows and buttercups, but when it is attached to her, it makes you think of a bright young lass who comes in with the other children every Sunday and of the loving family to which she belongs.

So the fatherhood of God is to be defined not by ancient or modern experiences of human fatherhood but by the revealed nature and character of the one who has revealed himself to us in his Son; like Father, like Son. That is the clear thrust of the teaching about the Father/Son relationship in John's Gospel. Negatively, it rejects all ideas of divine Fatherhood not mediated by Jesus: 'No one comes to the Father except through me' (John 14:6). Positively, it affirms that the nature and character of Jesus are a faithful and reliable human expression of the nature and character of the one who sent him: 'Whoever has seen me has seen the Father' (John 14:9).

To speak the language of the Lord's Prayer, the one to whom Jesus calls us to pray is 'Our Father *in heaven*', which means that he is Father in the heavenly way appropriate to his divine existence and not in the earthly way of human fathers with all the limitations of their 'createdness' and the corruption of their sins.

FATHER AND GENDER

The Christian tradition has always affirmed that the fatherhood of God implies no limitation of gender; the heavenly Father is not a male who requires a female to complement and complete him. The fourth-century Bishop Hilary of Poitiers famously said that the Son of God comes forth, 'from the womb of the Father', thus affirming that God's fatherhood includes and does not exclude his motherhood. He is the one single source and origin of all that is male and all that is female in the created order, so that women as much as men and men as much as women can find in him all they need to transform them into the living image of the motherly Father who made them. To come in prayer to such a Father is not to come to one whose gender might alienate us from him, but to the one who is the source and promise of life to us all.

This is the Father who in Jesus reveals himself not as the patriarchal tyrant but as the compassionate liberator, who calls both men
and women to close personal relationship with himself. Again and
again in the name of his Father Jesus rejects the culture that down-
graded women and he affirms his Father's will to liberate and affirm
them in their relationship with him and in their calling to serve him.
The way Jesus related to women is one of the outstanding features of
his ministry expressed in many different ways throughout the Gospel
stories, from his relationship to the Samaritan woman at the well
(John 4:6–30) through his affirming of the right of Mary of Bethany
to sit at his feet along with his male disciples (Luke 10:38–42) to his
commissioning of Mary Magdalene as the first apostolic messenger
of the good news of his resurrection (John 20:11–18).

It was, in fact, to Mary at the empty tomb that he spoke of the
God who is 'my Father and your Father' (John 20:17). Women as
much as men share in the hope and confidence that come when the
Spirit of the Son cries out *Abba* in their hearts and joyously declares
that they are the children and heirs of this Father God.

FATHER AND COVENANT

For Paul, as for ourselves, the God and Father of our Lord Jesus
Christ is also the God of Abraham, Isaac and Jacob, the God who
brought his people out of the land of Egypt to their freedom in
Canaan, whose name as given to Moses is Yahweh. The New Testament is the renewed covenant that this God makes with his people
—the fulfilment and completion of his original covenant that is
central to his relationship with Israel. The covenantal relationship is
defined in a single sentence that keeps recurring in the Old Testament scriptures: 'I will be your God and you shall be my people'
(Leviticus 26:12; Ezekiel 36:28). The first half of that sentence
affirms God's unbreakable promise to his people; the second half
is both promise and command: it involves on the one hand a
requirement that his people should answer the committed love in

which God gives himself to them with a responding love in which they give themselves to him, and on the other hand a guarantee that God will lead and empower them in a way that will ultimately ensure the fulfilment of the covenant, both in his love for them and their love for him.

The New Testament gospel is the crown and consummation of this covenant. In Jesus as the Father's Son, God becomes utterly and completely our God, but in Jesus as the Messiah King of Israel, God finds the human response that fulfils the covenant from the human side; Jesus is both God totally for humankind and human-kind totally for God, he is the one who loves the Lord his God with all his heart and soul and mind and strength, and loves his neigh-bour (including his crucifying enemies) all the way to the cross, so that in him the covenant is fulfilled from both sides.

To this God, who has consummated his covenant love in Christ and whose name is *Abba*, do we offer our prayers. To Jesus, *Abba* was the one whose will could be totally obeyed because his love could be totally trusted. In covenantal language, you could give yourself totally to him because you knew that he had given and would give himself totally to you.

Abba at Gethsemane

It is significant that the first appearance of the word *Abba* in the New Testament is not in Paul's letters but in Mark's account of Jesus' agonizing struggle in the garden of Gethsemane—the location of that ultimate and best school of prayer to which we shall find we have to return again and again: "'Abba, Father", he said, "everything is possible for you. Take this cup from me. Yet not what I will but what you will"' (Mark 14:36, NIV). The struggle that this prayer expresses is the evidence that the bitter cup of atoning suffering and death is not being forced on him; he has to take it up in his own willing hand. At the same time, Jesus knows that his Father's pur-poses, which can be fulfilled only by his suffering and death, cannot be deflected into an undemanding indulgence that would spare him. So, in his prayer, while he still shrinks from the horror before him, the shrinking yields to the willing obedience to go God's way even when it is leading straight to Calvary.

We engage with a Father who can be obeyed like this because he can be trusted like this, and that is the trust we shall find when we bring our prayers to *Abba*. We have to approach such prayers expecting to know the grace in which, with utter abandon, God will give himself to us and prove that he is our God, but also recognizing the demand implicit in such love that, as he has dealt with us, so in responsive obedience we should be ready to deal with him.

Generous grace and obedient response

Christian prayer takes its distinctive character first of all from being addressed to a God of such grace and generosity. In our prayers, we are invited to come to the Father who, in his liberating and gracious love, is totally committed to us and will do for us and require of us whatever it takes to bring us into full openness and obedient responsiveness to that love. So, even if the going is often quite hard in our relationship with *Abba*, we can take it and face it because the gospel gives us every reason to believe and trust in his forgiving mercy and the generous provisions of his transforming grace. If we know our Father's nature and character as his Son reveals it to us, we can be confident that if we ask him for bread he will not give us a stone (see Matthew 7:9).

Two Gospels give this promise a different spin. In Matthew, we find: 'If you then, who are evil, know how to give good gifts to your children, how much more will your Father in heaven give good gifts to those who ask him!' (Matthew 7:11)—here the emphasis is on God's readiness to meet our needs. Luke, however, puts it differently: 'How much more will the heavenly Father *give the Holy Spirit* to those who ask him!' (Luke 11:13)—the emphasis is on

God's readiness to give us not just his gifts but his Spirit, which is himself.

In response to our prayers, God will guide us into a life in Christ in which we receive God's life into ourselves, not to hold on to it for ourselves but to give it for and to others just as Jesus himself did on the cross. We pray in order that we become more and more open to receive what God wants to give us but also to offer that life on behalf of others: that is what it means to intercede.

Children and heirs

That is exactly what Paul means when he says that 'it is that very Spirit bearing witness with our spirit that we are children of God' (Romans 8:16). As we pray, the Spirit imparts to us and renews in us the assurance that just as God was, from start to finish, *Abba* to Jesus, so he will be, from start to finish, *Abba* to us, with all the glorious generosity and costly demands implied by contact with him. The passage emphasizes both: 'If [we are] children, then heirs, heirs of God and joint heirs with Christ' (v. 17). This is unbounded generosity; all that God gave to Jesus he will also give to us without limit or stint.

But read on: 'if, in fact, we suffer with him so that we may also be glorified with him' (v. 17). This shows the demanding nature of our relationship to *Abba*. The suffering and cost that sharing his love involves is not a contradiction or diminution of that love but, rather, its expression. To be the acknowledged, loved and favoured child of this Father is to be bound for the giving of Galilee and the suffering of Calvary and only so to come to the glory of Easter.

Provision and calling

To be embraced in the boundless generosity of God's love must mean for us to be progressively reshaped by the love into a responding generosity, and day by day in our exposure to God this reshaping is to be defined, accepted and empowered. The place of prayer is to be the place where we seek God's provision for us but also the place where we hear and are brought to the point of obeying God's calling to us—never the one without the other. To look for the provision while we are evading the calling is to take our prayers out of the garden of Gethsemane and the company of Jesus and to try to relocate them in a cosy nook of self-indulgence that we have made for ourselves.

We need to keep asking if our prayers are too centred on our own needs, or if there is in them an outgoing to the needs of others and to the miseries and perplexities of the world around us and a readiness to let ourselves be at least part of the means by which God will help those for whom we pray. It makes no sense to pray about the loneliness of a neighbour we seldom make time to visit or to agonize before God about the dangers of climate change while our own unchanged lifestyle continues to contribute to it. We are not exempt from the deceptions of our engrained self-indulgence just because we are on our knees before God; we need to soak ourselves in the greatness of his generosity until we perceive and repent of the littleness of our own.

It is also true the other way round—we shall never meet the demands of *Abba*'s love until we have sought and received the gifts of its generosity. I have come across people who have told me that they were taught never to ask God for anything for themselves. The self-effacing politeness which demands that you should never ask for anything at table but wait until it is offered to you has been turned into the rule of prayer. Our concern is with the needs of others and we leave it to God to notice our own. It is true indeed that our heavenly Father knows what we need before we ask him (see Matthew 6:8), but everything that Jesus and the Gospels say about prayer makes it clear that our dependence on God and our faith in his care for our lives in all their personal detail needs to be expressed and acknowledged; our confidence in him leads to specific requests and not just mute expectation. God's generosity is to be sought and not just taken for granted: '... how much more will your Father in heaven give good things *to those who ask him!*' (Matthew 7:11). In the asking is the confession that without his help we shall never make it on our own and the expression of our confidence that he cares enough to answer. To relate to *Abba* is always to ask for his care and always to answer his call.

ABBA AND HIS CHILDREN

The word *Abba* has one further implication for our praying—it is the word of a small child. You can hear that from the sound of it, and, if you go to Israel today, you will hear little children using it to greet their dads. What such a small child asks will be attended to, not because of its eloquence or intrinsic persuasiveness, but because the child belongs to the family loved by the father, so he can understand what she is saying even if she uses the most inexpert and fumbling words. A lawyer presenting a case to a judge has to get his arguments right if he is going to win; a petitioner to a king has to marshal his reasons and his inducements if he is going to prevail. But the child is listened to in the family circle, not because she is eloquent or convincing, but just because she is loved.

There are many valid justifications for a concern for good liturgy to guide the worship of the church, but such a concern and our attachment to preferred liturgies, whether ancient or modern, must not be allowed to mask the basic simplicity of what is happening when we pray, even if our prayer is expressed in forms that liturgical experts would dismiss and deplore. An excessive obsession with liturgical correctness can make it harder for ordinary people to pray their own prayers, because they might think that they are not doing it correctly. Jesus himself warns us of the dangers of an excessive preoccupation with the outward forms of our prayers: 'When you are praying, do not heap up empty phrases as the Gentiles do; because they think that they will be heard because of their many words. Do not be like them, for your Father knows what you need before you ask him' (Matthew 6:7–8). The meeting of person with person, the coming together of loving Father with needy child—that is the inviting and encouraging simplicity at the heart of it all: *Abba* knows, *Abba* cares, *Abba* gives.

PRAYING WITH THE SON

If God the Father is the one *to* whom we pray, God the Son is the enabling partner of our praying. That is the clear implication of what Paul says in Romans 8:34 when he speaks of the ascended Christ '… who is at the right hand of God, who indeed intercedes for us.' When we pray on earth we have a divine companion who is praying to the Father on our behalf in all the mysterious intimacy of their love for each other. The right hand of God is the place of power— 'All authority in heaven and on earth has been given to me' (Matthew 28:18)—but the place of power is also the place of prayer; the secret of the Lord's continuing power is the Lord's continuous intercession. This is a king indeed, but a king on his knees, a king who prays.

THE PRAYING PRIEST

In Romans 8 Paul makes no more than a passing reference to the intercession of the ascended Christ, but it is of course a central theme of the letter to the Hebrews. The writer of that letter—almost certainly not Paul—teaches that Christ's once-for-all sacrifice on the cross has perpetual power because it is the basis of his perpetual high-priestly intercession in heaven; he was crucified only once but his unique self-giving on Calvary is offered for ever to the Father on our behalf: 'He holds his priesthood permanently, because he continues for ever. Consequently he is able for all time to save those who approach God through him, *since he always lives to make intercession for them*' (Hebrews 7:24–25). If heaven is a place of praise in the book of Revelation, in Hebrews it is a place of prayer: the two are not contradictory but complementary and all who join in the one join in the other as well.

The power of intercession

All this tells us a great deal about intercession, first about Christ's and then about our own. Christ's perpetual intercession is based upon and continuous with his unique sacrifice, and the one explains the other. They are both, in their different ways, actions in which the same Christ identifies himself with the needs and perils of others in order that he may offer himself on behalf of these others to God.

On the cross, Jesus shoulders and takes on himself the whole mess of the sinful human situation, overcomes the evil of it by the identifying love that he brings into it and opens it all up to God by offering himself to his Father from the midst of it. On the third day the Father answers the self-offering prayer of the cross by raising his Son from the dead and so affirms that this identifying and interceding love is stronger than all the accumulated and crucifying evil of the world.

That interceding identification, made once for all in the agony of Calvary, is continued in the intercession of the High Priest in heaven, where Christ who has died for us continues to offer himself to the Father on our behalf: 'Therefore he had to become like his brothers and sisters in every respect, so that he might be a merciful and faithful high priest in the service of God, to make a sacrifice of atonement for the sins of the people. Because he himself was tested by what he suffered, he is able to help those who are being tested' (Hebrews 2:17).

Intercession—Christ's and ours

The connection between Calvary and intercession shows us what a costly business it is. Intercessory prayer is never a quick run through a list of needy people and causes; it always involves a measure of real identification with those for whom we pray, so that we may be in a position to offer these others in love to God.

We nevertheless need to remember that, although our intercession must mirror the intercession of Jesus, it can never be equivalent to it, far less take its place. His unique calling as the incarnate Son of God is to take on himself and to offer to his Father the whole need of the whole world. We are neither able nor called to carry such a burden. What he does universally and continuously, we are called to do only partially and specifically. His ability to identify with sinners and sufferers is as unbounded as the love of God, which is incarnate in him: he prays for everybody always while we can pray only for some people sometimes. If we take on too much, we shall either fail to identify with it or be broken down by the weight of it.

We had friends who had a countrywide healing ministry, and they were besieged by people asking them to pray for them. They would answer with great wisdom, 'Yes we will—once, and then see if God wants us to go on for a week or a month or a year.'

Jesus allocates to different people different ways and degrees of sharing in his ministry of intercession and the identification with people that it requires. It is one thing to pray once for somebody whose need has caught our attention and evoked our sympathy and quite another to commit ourselves over the long term to a deep, informed and concerned intercession for a person and a situation that God has laid on our hearts. There is a place for both and for many degrees of involvement in between, and there is a godly wisdom that knows what is too little and what is too much in any given case.

Why intercession works

Intercession works because, as the cross shows, self-offering of all kinds is the means by which God's recreating power and love are released into the world. Intercession is not the art of persuading a reluctant God to do what he would otherwise be unwilling to do, any more than the cross is a matter of persuading an angry God to forgive. The truth is, rather, that the intercession of Christ is the means by which God's mercy, healing, power and guidance can flow to those for whom he prays, so that the Father's hands can grip them and shape their hearts, their relationships and their circumstances in a way that furthers his purposes for them.

Where a Christian intercessor gives herself in prayer on behalf of another, that act of self-giving, limited and partial as it may be, is caught up into the total self-giving of Christ, the High Priest, and becomes the mysterious means by which the Father's love is made active in those who are receiving prayer. Christ's intercession is, in more senses than one, always crucial, and our prayers are effective only when they are consonant with and dependent upon his. He is in all things the only Saviour and our praying is saved from the *astheneia* that always afflicts it by his perfect prayer offered on behalf of all who pray along with him. That is why it is no empty formality but the very heart of the matter that Christians pray always and only 'through Jesus Christ our Lord'.

Christ prevails when we fail

The glory of it is that his prayers persist and prevail even when ours fail and fall silent. He prays for us even if nobody else does and even when we have stopped praying for ourselves. When Jesus announces that one of his disciples is going to betray him, Peter is quick and confident in his protestations of unlimited loyalty and will not heed Jesus' warning that he is going to deny his Lord before the night is out. But Jesus says, 'Simon, Simon, listen! Satan had demanded to sift all of you like wheat, *but I have prayed for you that your own faith may not fail*; and you, when once you have turned back, strengthen your brothers' (Luke 22:31–32).

What stands between Peter and total shipwreck is not his own pledged loyalty in which he is vainly putting his trust, but the intercession of Jesus: 'I have prayed for you.' That is why, when his proud promises collapse in craven cowardice, he can still be reintegrated into Christ's purposes and, in spite of his own weakness, be enabled to become a strength to his brother apostles. He is saved from himself by the intercession of Jesus.

In our prayer life we all have our own collapses and denials, even if they are more secret than Peter's. There are times of illness and depression when anything like a flourishing prayer life becomes nearly impossible, and we have to ask others to pray for us when we have no heart or energy to do it for ourselves. There are days of disappointment when something we had eagerly desired and sought from God is not given to us; the illness we dreaded has happened, the bereavement we asked to be spared has come, and we are left confused and for the moment faithless, under the surface angry and disillusioned that God who promised so much has delivered so little. All the doors of heaven seem to have been slammed in our faces. In such an unpropitious environment prayer can easily collapse into formality or silence.

Even in these times of paralysis, our names and our needs are still presented faithfully and tirelessly by the great High Priest who has himself known the depths of abandonment and so can empathize with us in such moments. He prays us through the dark night to a mysterious resourcing and reviving of faith, and to the restoration of relationship that makes our own prayer once again possible and hopeful so that we are ushered into a new Easter with God. Our occasional prayerlessness will not be final or fatal because the prayer of the ascended Jesus will prevail on our behalf and awaken us again to the love of God for us.

The prayer of the incarnate Christ who makes intercession for his people and the world at the right hand of the Father is the prototype of Christian praying, its meaning and its power. His giving himself for us, first on the cross and then in the mystery of his ascended presence with the Father, is the means by which God's love reaches

God's world. That prayer is perpetual and powerful, and it is our calling and our privilege to pray in, with and through Christ so that also through us God's blessings may flow.

Such a contemplation of the praying High Priest will lead to great gratitude and rejoicing that we have such a friend at the heavenly court to represent us before the Father. At the same time, as we compare the meagreness of our intercessory efforts to the completeness and intensity of the self-giving that undergirds his, it will arouse in us a desire to pray better and to pray more.

PRAYING IN THE SPIRIT

This leads us straight to the third trinitarian dimension of prayer emphasized by Paul in verses that describe the action of the Holy Spirit in our praying in a way not paralleled in the rest of the New Testament: 'Likewise the Spirit helps us in our weakness... that very Spirit intercedes with sighs too deep for words. And God, who searches the heart, knows what is the mind of the Spirit, *because the Spirit intercedes for the saints according to the will of God*' (Romans 8:26–27). We pray *to* the Father, we pray *with* the Son, but we also pray *in* the Spirit or, rather, as Paul puts it here, the Spirit prays in us.

THE DISTINCTIVE WORK OF THE SPIRIT

We should notice that what Paul is saying here about the distinctive work of the Spirit in our prayers is consonant with what he and the other New Testament writers, in particular John, say about the work of the Spirit in its relation to the work of the Son. It can be summed up by saying that what the Son does *for* us, the Spirit then does *in* us. In the familiar words of the Grace, Paul uses the phrase the 'fellowship of the Holy Spirit' (2 Corinthians 13:14, NIV). The original Greek word is *koinonia*, a far richer word than the English 'fellowship', which speaks of our sharing participation in the grace of the Lord Jesus Christ and the love of God the Father. Through the Spirit all that originally belongs to the Father and the Son belongs to us as well; what is theirs becomes ours.

It is made even more explicit in what Jesus says about the Spirit in John's Gospel: 'He will glorify me, because he will take what is mine and declare it to you' (John 16:14). Jesus promises that, through the activity of the Spirit, all that constitutes Jesus' life and relationships will begin to constitute our life and relationships also. The Spirit will take the truth, the love, the power, the sonship, the remade humanity that is there for us, but originally beyond our reach in Jesus, and will impart them all to us. We shall then begin to live out of his truth, to love with his love, to operate with his power and to be human in the way that he is human, in restored relationships with God and with one another.

The intercessor within

The life of Jesus, both on earth and in heaven, comes to a climax in the saving intercession in which he offers himself on our behalf to the Father; therefore the Spirit, who makes us participators in all he does, enables us to participate also in his intercession. What Paul is saying in effect in Romans 8:26–27 (when read in conjunction with Romans 8:34) is that the Spirit takes the perfect prayer that Jesus offers in heaven and prays it again deep down in the hearts of his praying people.

The commentators have quite a field day discussing what precisely Paul meant by saying that the Spirit intercedes 'with sighs too deep for words' (v. 26). Gordon Fee,[8] speaking out of the Pentecostal tradition, makes a credible case for finding here a reference to speaking with tongues but admits that the Greek adjective *alaletos* means 'speechless' or 'wordless'. This would seem to rule out tongues, which would certainly involve a different kind of speaking and a different form of words.

For our purposes we need to see only that, whatever his precise meaning, Paul is here directing us to the Spirit who, deep down inside us, is crying to God on our behalf. In those who have this gift, it may express itself in tongues on an outward level, but it is also happening without need for any words in us at all.

THE PRAYING SPIRIT

André Louf, in his great book *Teach us to Pray*, tells us that the prayer of the Spirit is a central if sometimes unnoticed ingredient that is with us right from the start of our Christian life: 'From then on in the profoundest depths of the self, we have a continuing contact with God. God's Holy Spirit has taken us over, has assumed complete possession of us; he has become breath of our breath and Spirit of our spirit. He takes our heart in tow and turns it towards God... All the time... the Spirit is calling within us and he prays *Abba*, Father, with supplications and sighs that cannot be put into words but never for an instant cease within our hearts.'[9]

This is indeed mysterious and wonderful, and to probe even a little into what Paul is saying here is to discover a source of encouragement and richness that can transform our whole approach to our praying.

Prayer as given

It underlines that prayer is a *gift* before it is a *task*. We do not have to produce it out of our own resources, because the Spirit brings into our praying the praying of Jesus to the Father and prays it on our behalf at the depths of our being. Our business therefore is to tap into the prayer of the Spirit for all the things and people for whom we seek God's help.

Praying perfected

Also, the prayer of the Spirit is the *perfect prayer*, because 'the Spirit intercedes for the saints according to the will of God' (Romans 8:27). On the surface level, because of our weakness, we may be praying for the wrong thing in the wrong way; but that is not the end of the matter, because on the level of the Spirit the right prayer in the right way is already being offered, and to that the Father listens and responds. This finally puts into perspective and overcomes all those feelings of incompetence that Paul confesses and that we know only too well. In the very place where we may be praying badly, the Spirit is present and is praying well.

Praying transformed

It follows from this that our poor prayer can be changed and transformed when we are tuned in to the wavelength of the Spirit. We all start by asking for what in our best judgment we see to be best for a person or situation. But in the very act of our praying, the prayer of the Spirit can surface into it and teach us what we should be asking and give us the faith that God will hear and answer.

We saw this happening in Paul's prayer about his thorn in the flesh when he stopped asking to have it removed because he realized that God could work better with it than without it. We can see it happening in a different way in some of the Psalms—a prayer of despairing complaint against God is quite abruptly and without explanation replaced by a prayer of abounding hope and trust in the same God. The external circumstances have not changed, but the Spirit has broken through in the praying and the psalmist's attitude to the situation has changed completely.

That happens most remarkably in Jesus' own prayer in Gethsemane, which he begins by asking what his human insight and even more his human dread lead him to ask: 'Let this cup pass from me' (Matthew 26:39). But as he goes on praying, the Spirit, who in all his fullness dwells within him, lets him see that the bitter cup he shrinks from has to be drunk to its last dregs if the Father's saving purpose is to be fulfilled, and the prayer changes: 'If this [cup] cannot pass unless I drink it, your will be done' (v. 42).

So with us, both the content and the mood of our praying can be changed as we pray. We can come to see that the way we quite rightly started asking is not the way God wants to go; we gain new insights into how he wants to handle what we bring to him, and as we discern his will, the Spirit overcomes our reluctance and our own will swings round to affirm it. In our prayers for sick people, for example, the prayer for healing can turn into the prayer of relinquishment and equally the prayer of relinquishment can turn into the prayer for healing.

TUNING IN TO THE SPIRIT

Such a process can happen only when we have grown into a listening maturity that has learned to distinguish the voice of the Spirit from the clamour of our own desires and all the other voices that deafen our ears and distract our attention. It needs a lot of experience to do that well and there will inevitably be mistakes along the way.

In all this, it is vital to remember that the prayer of the Spirit echoes the prayer of Jesus; we shall be able to hear the voice of the Spirit in our hearts only when we are listening to the voice of Jesus in the gospel.

The better we know Jesus in the scriptures, in the sacraments, in the liturgical worship of the church, which reflect a long tradition of this kind of listening, the better we shall be able to discern what the Spirit is praying within us with regard to specific needs and situations, especially if we are able to submit our individual discernments to those who are praying with us in the body of Christ.

On a day-to-day basis, reading the scriptures and praying are two of the things that God has joined together and that we tear apart at our peril. You will never know what the Spirit is saying in your heart until you know what the Lord is saying in his word.

Even so, the most mature of us will sometimes get it wrong on the surface level, where we are often confused and perplexed. Our comfort and confidence is that at the heart level the Spirit is getting it right and offering on our behalf the prayer the Father can answer and use to bless those who are brought to him through it.

ENDING WITH BLESSING

As we have explored the implications of what Paul says about prayer in Romans 8, we have come to see that to pray *to* the Father, *with* the Son and *in* the Spirit is nothing less than to be wonderfully caught up into the self-giving love that constitutes the trinitarian life of God and that is a source of blessing to all who are opened up to it.

We may then appropriately end this chapter with our own trinitarian blessing:

Blessed be Abba, Father who loves us, hears us and answers our prayers.

Blessed be Jesus, the Son of God, who loved us and gave himself for us once on the cross and now offers himself on our behalf before the Father.

Blessed be the Holy Spirit of God who draws us into the intercession of Christ and prays with us his perfect prayer in our hearts.

✥

――――――― *Chapter Four* ―――――――

PAUL AND THE PRACTICE OF PRAYER

Key Passage: Philippians 4:4-7

As we move from the long passage in Romans 8, which has been the starting point of our first three chapters, to these short, snappy verses in Philippians, the first thing to notice is that here the mood of the dominant verbs changes from the indicative to the imperative, in other words, from statements to commands. In Romans we learnt that prayer is a gift God gives to us, an intercession that the ascended Christ makes for us and the Spirit offers from deep within us. These are the rich resources for our praying, which enable us to participate in the interchanges of love and life that constitute the being of the triune God who is Father, Son and Holy Spirit.

AN IMPERATIVE INVITATION

Now, however, the imperatives of this passage move us on from the wondering and thankful contemplation of such mysteries and invite us not just to think about them, but actually to do the things that will involve us in them and make them real for us. We are invited to take practical steps to lead us out of worrying into rejoicing, to enter into fulfilled relationships with God and other people, here described as 'the peace that passes all understanding' (see Philippians 4:7), by finding a time and a place to make our requests known to God in a way that recognizes with thanksgiving all he has already given to us and takes all the needs that arise in our lives and opens them up to him: '... in everything by prayer and supplication with thanksgiving let your requests be made known to God' (v. 6).

So, summarized, the invitation opens the attractive prospect of unlimited access to God's resources, as we have already explored them. However, the invitation has to be accepted by our taking the deliberate practical steps of making and maintaining room in our lives for these things. We have to find, each in our own way, time and space for personal exposure to the love of *Abba* and for listening and tuning in to the prayer of Christ as it is echoed by the Spirit deep down in our hearts—and that can be quite hard.

ARROWS IN EMERGENCIES

Surveys show that even in our secular society many more people than we might have imagined say that they pray, but when you get near enough to ask them what this means in practice, it often amounts to little more than arrow prayers for help in the midst of some emergency or a few snatched moments of quiet on a bus or commuter train on the way to work in the morning.

Such minimal praying is by no means to be despised, not least because God does not despise it and his grace can find a way even through a door that is open only a little and for a moment. But if help can come through such a minimal opening, how much more could it come if the moment became half an hour and the prayer for one pressing need was extended to offer all the varied concerns of a whole life to God? That is what Paul is after when we says, 'in everything let your requests be made known to God' (v. 6).

First to find and then to keep that time takes determination and a wisdom to know when and where and how long will best suit our own personality and circumstances. It is a time that, even when found, will be under constant attack from all the other matters and people clamouring for our attention and dissipating our concentration.

DISINCLINATION AND DISCIPLINE

Time for praying is threatened even more by the strange disinclination to expose ourselves to God, which keeps coming back even when we have found that seeking his presence is a source of joy and confidence. Just because he has answered past prayers, we are not automatically ready to bring him more. His love may be new every morning, but so is our reluctance to come to him, and it takes the discipline of a pledged routine firmly anchored in our daily timetable to bring us to our knees in his presence. This reluctance is felt not just by people in the midst of crowded lives but also by religious professionals who know all about the promises attached to prayer but still often struggle to find time and inclination to claim them. Even when we are retired and have lots of time at our disposal, it can still be an effort to devote a significant part of it to God.

When we are looking hard-headedly at our daily schedule and carving out time for prayer, the larks perhaps at the start of the day, the owls at the end, we are in fact dealing with very fundamental issues of where our relationship to God comes in the hierarchy of the priorities that rule our lives. If he has first place in our hearts, he will have first place in our timetable; if he is first, then time for him will be more important than time for sleep or time for TV. He will have the first claim on the hours that are at our disposal.

Our time for prayer may be short, but it will be vital. To start with, 15 minutes may be enough, but the more we engage with God the more time we will want to give him; time spent with him will start to expand and will be stretched out to be long enough for us to tell all that is on our hearts and to listen for his word of pardon, of guidance and of grace. Prayer can indeed be hard to start, but when you have found God in it, it can also be hard to stop.

WE AND 'I-THOU'

The truth is that the short time we keep *for* God can transform the rest of our lives into time shared *with* God. The German theologian Heribert Mühlen used to say that there are two kinds of personal relationships that can fill our days—'we' times and 'I-Thou' times—and that all our close and continuous relationships have to find time for both.[10]

Take for example a typical husband and wife; for most of the time they are living alongside each other as 'we', sharing the chores, raising the children, facing the issues affecting them, offering hospitality to friends who come to them. But if their relationship is to remain healthy and fruitful, there have to be moments when, instead of standing side by side as 'we', dealing together with all that life brings them, they have to turn away from all the external issues and face each other. Room has to be made for a renewal and a purification of their relationship with each other, a making and a remaking of the love that originally brought them together. The bond that enables them to function as 'we' is repaired and strengthened in what is often nowadays called the 'quality time' that they keep for themselves, the 'I-Thou' exchange between them in which each is affirmed and renewed. In these moments they shut out everybody else so that they may be able again to be of use to everybody else. If their 'I-Thou' relationship is neglected and allowed to go wrong, they will be increasingly disabled from the joint service and witness to their children, their friends and their world to which as 'we' they are called.

These are the two dimensions that constitute healthy relationships, not just in marriage but also in the whole richness of our personal dealings with one another. Without the co-operative 'we', life loses its purpose and its drive; without the intimate 'I-Thou', it loses its warmth and its worth and we are left in the isolation and loneliness in which we can work only with ourselves and talk only to ourselves. As it is in our relationships with one another, so it is also in our relationship with God. To work with him is our public calling, but to give to him and to receive from him is our intimate privilege; we can be fruitful as God's fellow workers only when we are faithful in turning from the tasks of the kingdom and sharing life with the king of the kingdom.

When Jesus chose his twelve disciples, his purpose was for them 'to be with him and to be sent out to proclaim the message and to have authority to cast out demons' (Mark 3:14–15). It is quite clear that their exercise of the authority he shared with them was totally dependent on their constantly keeping company with him and being in that way open to all he had to give them. If they lost touch with him, they would soon be unable to deliver his message and would lose their power to cope with the demonic forces that stood in their path. They could face the world in solidarity with Jesus only if they knew how to turn their backs on the world to be alone with Jesus, to be taught, forgiven, reorientated, guided and strengthened by their submission to him. It is pointless to clatter dishes in Martha's kitchen because you want to serve Jesus if it distracts and keeps you from sitting with Mary at Jesus' feet (see Luke 10:38–41).

The pressures of our busy world and the restlessness it provokes in our own personal lives make it hard for us to be still enough to know that God is God. We want to do things for Jesus without making room to be with Jesus, with the result that we know neither what priorities he has for us nor what resources he can supply to us. All the time the call to worship is drowned out by the demands of work or leisure, so that many of us have an unsatisfied need to listen to Jesus when he tells us to '... go into your room and shut the door and pray to your Father who is in secret, and your Father who sees in secret will reward you' (Matthew 6:6). What happens in the intimacy of the 'I-Thou' of prayer will have its public effects in the 'we' world of our activity in all the networks to which we belong.

INVITATION AND PROMISE

The importance of the verses of Paul in Philippians 4:4–7 is that they instruct us and promise us what will happen when we have escaped from the clamour around us into the quiet room where the door is shut for a while and prayer can begin.

If we look more closely at the verses in which Paul sets out the content of the time we spend with God, we can see that they consist of several commands sandwiched between two statements. The first statement, 'the Lord is near' (v. 5), outlines the presupposition from which our prayer can start; the second, 'the peace of God... will guard your hearts and your minds in Christ Jesus' (v. 7), holds out the promise that will be fulfilled as we pray, and the various commands indicate the way from the one to the other.

THE NEARNESS OF GOD

The conviction that the Lord is near makes our prayer possible and profitable. Because he is near, he can be spoken to; because he is the lovingly responsive Lord Jesus shows him to be, he is able and willing to respond to what we say to him. It is the realization of this that makes my prayer not a cry of desperation to an unknown deity who may or may not pay any attention to it, but, rather, a confident appeal to the God and Father of our Lord Jesus Christ who, one way or another, will answer me in his love.

The word 'near' is worth staying with for a little. To say that someone is near is to say that he is available and not remote, but also that he is different from me and not identical to me. As we have already noted in Chapter One, Christian prayer is quintessentially dialogical; it is an act of communication and self-giving between two parties who are inexpressibly close to each other but at the same time personally distinct from each other. When I pray, I am not left alone with myself to meditate on my own thoughts or explore the depths of my own being. Between God and me there is a space allowing him the freedom to give himself to me and me the freedom to give myself to him. The nearness ensures that we are within speaking distance of each other, but it also ensures that we each remain ourselves in the integrity of our personal freedom.

OUR PRAYER AND OUR FREEDOM

On the one hand, prayer does not involve the overcoming of our humanity by God's divinity. The imperatives of our passage, 'rejoice' (v. 4), 'let your requests be made known to God' (v. 6) emphasize that our prayer is undertaken in the human freedom that God gives to and respects in us because, in this freedom, we reflect the freedom that characterizes the life of God.

Prayer, as we have seen in Romans 8, is prompted, motivated and guided by the Spirit, but, at the end of the day, it is you and I and nobody else who have to take responsibility for the way we receive the gift of prayer given to us by the Spirit. Are we ourselves prepared to make space in our lives to tune in to the prayer the Spirit is offering deep down in our hearts and thus make it our own? If Romans 8:26 offers us a gift, the imperatives of Philippians 4 summon us to the task of framing a regime of prayer to enable us to claim and receive this gift. God's gifts, here as elsewhere, do not abolish the need for human response but, rather, motivate and inspire it. Precisely because the Spirit prays in us, we have to take the steps enabling us to pray in the Spirit.

PRAYER AND GOD'S FREEDOM

On the other hand, it is equally clear that if prayer is not the overcoming of the human by the divine, still less is it the overcoming of the divine by the human. If, in his nearness to us, God respects our freedom, how much more, in our nearness to him, are we to respect his.

Looking back on what happened in the charismatic renewal, I can see how easy it was for a renewed faith in the power and generosity of God to give us what we asked to turn into a search for techniques for extracting whatever we wanted from God in terms of health and happiness and even sometimes money. Prayer is not a self-seeking enterprise of finding ways to bend God's will to ours. The one who is near us is from first to last the Lord; our prayer is an appeal to that Lordship but never an encroachment upon it. The difference between petition and manipulation is that the one respects and the other obscures God's freedom—his freedom to respond to our prayers not as we see fit but as he thinks right, and to keep his promises to us at times and in ways of his own appointing rather than of our choosing.

A DIALOGUE WITH A LIVING GOD

Day to day in the practice of prayer, I find that I have to continually remind myself of the dialogical character of what I am doing, of the nearness of the God with whom I am dealing (in Paul's terminology) or, in the language of sacramental theology, of his real presence with me. I am not shut up in a self-contained monologue in which I am thinking through the situations that concern me and trying to decide what best can bedone about them.

Everyone who prays knows what a constant temptation that can be, but everyone who prays to the Father in the name of the Son and in the power of the Spirit also knows that the whole heart of the enterprise in which we are engaged is getting things out of our incompetent hands and into the mighty hands of God, to transfer them from the areas of our own concern (which are often imposs-ible to deal with) and into the realm of the mighty love that first made, then sustained and finally redeemed the world. So, when I pray, I have to take my bearings not from what I think of issues or people but rather from what *he* is telling me about them in the light of the gospel, and then I have to wait and watch to see in the working out of events what his response to them might be. In other words, my prayers need to be constantly moved out from self-absorbed meditation into God-orientated intercession, which finds its hope and confidence in the God who is able and has promised to listen to me and, in Paul's words in another letter, to do for me far more than I could ask or think (see Ephesians 3:20).

CONVICTION AND EMOTION

The presupposition of that kind of praying is precisely the conviction that the Lord is near. It is most important to recognize here, and in all that follows, that we are speaking the language of conviction rather than emotion. I pray as one who is in the presence of God, not because I feel he is close but because I have been convinced by the gospel that it is so. On the level of feeling, I may be stone cold, with my sceptical mind crying out that the whole enterprise of prayer is bogus because there is nobody there to respond to it.

Yet, at the same time, underneath and in contradiction to that, there is the believing bit of me, which holds on to the promises of God, promises convincing enough to motivate me to defy my scepticism, my disappointment and even sometimes my depression. To revert to Romans 8, I am still aware of the witness of the Holy Spirit who, whatever the state of my feelings, continues to cry *Abba* in the depths of my being and assures me that I will be heard because in Christ I am God's child and the rightful inheritor of all his riches. That is why much prayer is indeed a battle of conviction against experience, of faith against feeling and therefore falls again under the category of 'I believe; help my unbelief!' (Mark 9:24). Our continuing to pray in such circumstances is a sign that trembling faith rather than negative feeling is having its way.

WHEN PERSONAL PRAYER IS IMPOSSIBLE

Within that conflict there may indeed be moments when we are so debilitated and depressed, either by what has befallen us or by the collapse of our internal psychological equilibrium, that our faith can for the moment no longer move us to pray and the witness of the Spirit is rendered inaudible by the voices of fear, anger, resentment and despair shouting so loudly that we cannot hear anything else. In times like this, we have to remember that faith has a corporate as well as a personal dimension. When we cannot come for ourselves, our need and our misery can be brought into the presence of God by the prayers of other people who still believe when we cannot, who will hold us faithfully before God until the storm subsides and personal faith revives and we can pray ourselves once more. Until that happens, we have to seek and rely on the intercessions of others and above all on the prayer of the great High Priest who continues to pray for us by name when we have stopped praying for ourselves: 'Simon,... I have prayed for you that your own faith may not fail' (Luke 22:31–32).

FAITH KINDLES FEELING

Often and happily, however, the battle goes the other way—rather than faith being overwhelmed by feeling, emotion follows faith. A conviction of the nearness of God opens the door to a real sense of the presence of God.

My emotional tone is never at its most vibrant first thing in the morning, as I am by nature an owl rather than a lark. I often approach the time reserved for prayer after breakfast with a maximum of reluctance and a minimum of expectation. It looks at the start like a ritual duty to be faithfully performed rather than a life-enhancing encounter with the living Lord. It seldom feels like that at the end; somewhere in the midst of the process the light shines and the fire falls, not often in the form of a major experience of renewal, but more in terms of a word of scripture that wants to be embraced, a realization that something which happened yesterday was in fact God's answer to a long-offered prayer, a sense that a burden I had initially has been taken away from me and is now being carried on broader shoulders, an insight that changes my attitude to the way I face the day, or a call to move up to the top of my agenda something that I had been giving a much lower priority or none at all. Very often when, as I frequently do, I swing my chair round to look into the face of the Christ in the icon on the wall, I can see through the picture to the presence. The little room where I work and play computer games has become an awesome Bethel where with Jacob I am left saying, 'Surely the Lord is in this place—and I did not know it' (Genesis 28:16). I go out from it to face the day in the quiet but deep perception that the Lord is near. In the act of prayer, faith has enlightened feeling, conviction has led to encounter, the dullness of emotion that presumed his absence has given way to the warmth of gratitude that recognizes his presence.

HOW FAITH CAN FLOURISH

If authentic prayer depends on the conviction of faith in the presence of God, then an essential ingredient of prayer is an openness to everything that builds up this faith. In the liturgical provision that churches make for daily prayer, whether corporate or individual, the reading of scripture and especially of the psalms has a pre-eminent place. A persistent theme of the psalms is that when we dwell on what God has done for his people in the past, we shall grow in confidence and hope for what he will do for us in the future, and this gives prayer its reality. In what God has done in the past, we have the revelation and the promise of what he will do in the present and in the future.

As we open ourselves to the story of God's dealings with others in the past, we shall grow in faith that, as he was near to them, he will also be near to us, and what he did for them to meet their need in their day, he will also do for us in ours. As we read of the Spirit who bore witness to Paul and his people that they were the children of *Abba*, so we shall be able to hear again the same Spirit making the same witness to us. Scripture begets faith and faith begets prayer, and we are not to pull them apart. God in his grace hears cries of desperation, but to enter into the depths of our relationship with him we have to nourish the faith day by day that convinces us of his nearness.

ALWAYS REJOICING

When we turn from Paul's statement, 'the Lord is near' (Philippians 4:5), to his command, 'Rejoice in the Lord always; again I say, Rejoice' (v. 4), the distinction between the convictions of our faith and the responsiveness of our feelings can be seen to be even more important. We need to see first of all that Paul is not recommending that we cultivate a state of uninterrupted emotional exuberance. This could only occasionally be genuine, given the natural ebb and flow of our feelings, and could easily become an evasion of the hard realities around us by escaping into a world of religious fantasy.

It is easy to see that Paul was not promoting anything of this kind from the way he speaks about rejoicing in the rest of his letters. The rejoicing he recommends emerges, not when he closes his eyes to the suffering that seems to make it impossible but, rather, when he faces suffering head on. He speaks of how 'we also rejoice in our sufferings, because we know that suffering produces perseverance; perseverance, character; and character, hope' (Romans 5:3, NIV). Earlier in Philippians, he says that he rejoices in his imprisonment in Rome because his removal from the church scene has stirred up more people to proclaim the gospel (1:15–19). In Philippi, when Paul and Silas were in prison smarting from a fresh beating with rods, about midnight Paul and Silas were praying and singing hymns to God (Acts 16:25), just before an earthquake set them free and converted their jailer.

The evidence points to a joy that defies rather than denies suffering, that can come to us not in the good days, when everything is going well and rejoicing is easy, but precisely in the bad days, when things could not be worse and on the natural level there seems little to rejoice about.

REJOICING IN THE LORD

Yet, as Paul shows so clearly, even at these times a joy can break into us that does not have its source in the state of things around us or the emotional response we naturally make to them, but in the nature and the character of God to whom we expose ourselves in our prayers: it is *in the Lord* that we are to rejoice always, taking our bearings not from what is happening to us or to others, but from the nearness of God to us, especially as we confront all the things challenging his love for us and his power to help us.

For Paul, the Lord is always the Lord Jesus Christ who, on his cross, penetrated to the very depths of suffering and death and, in his resurrection, opened from these impossible places a new door into the reversal of all such areas; so that it is life and not death, hope and not despair, health and not illness, love and not hate, goodness and not evil that have the last word in all the places of suffering to which we allow the Lord entry.

To pray, especially in circumstances of deep distress, is to come to the one who has taken on all our suffering and will make it, against all the odds, the place where his life is given and his promises are kept. To pray to God is to open yourself to see the first glimmering of Easter morning, to hear the rustle of resurrection and therefore to lift up your heart in a God-grounded hope that, out of present sorrow, there is a road to future joy , so that in prayer you look at the situation with fresh eyes and ask God to show you the place where the road to resurrection might start.

PAUL AND THE PRACTICE OF PRAYER

JOY AS GIFT

Paul also describes the joy he speaks of in Philippians as a fruit of the Holy Spirit in Galatians 5:22. As we have already seen, the distinctive work of the Spirit is to 'take what is mine and declare it to you' (John 16:14), to connect what Christ has done for us in the cross and resurrection to whatever is happening in our lives at the present moment.

Such a connection happens more in the mysterious exchanges of our praying than it does in the thinking out of our theology. When I bring the issues undermining my life or the lives of other people or societies into contact with the living and reigning Lord Jesus, as he makes himself real to me in the Spirit, I shall be able to enter into the hope that rejoices in what the Lord will be able to do in such circumstances, which are threatening and deadly without him. In ths way, I can at least approach what it might mean to rejoice in the Lord—always!

STARTING WITH GOD

Such prayer, if it is to result in joy, must start with God. If it is not to sink in a sea of sadness, it must not start with a miserable recollection of our sins or a heavy recital of our needs or the agonies of the world but, rather, with God who in Christ will forgive our sins and can be relied upon to meet our needs. Christ has identified himself on the cross with the pain and agony of the world and has overcome them in the resurrection, so we can approach these things with confidence in the God who has shown himself able to both bear and overcome them.

That is the way the Lord's Prayer starts and indeed proceeds for a good half of its length. Before we ask for provision of bread, pardon for sin or protection from evil, we honour God who bears the name of Father, who has a fatherly rule that he will exercise and a fatherly will that in the end prevails. Having thus aligned ourselves with him, we have plugged into the source of the faith that bread will be given, sin will be forgiven and evil will be overthrown. Start with God and you start with faith, which begets hope and anticipates with joy what God will do for us. Start anywhere else and there is a real danger that faith will founder, hope will fail and there will be no joy in the Lord.

When I was ministering in Northern Ireland, I used to go once a month to an ecumenical healing service that totally failed to show the joy and confidence I have been talking about and was lugubrious, heavy and hopeless from start to finish—the most unlikely atmosphere in which any healing was likely to happen. The service was, for that very reason, nearly on its last legs with only the neurotic and the arthritic continuing to come—the fate, alas, of many such services.

I used to ask myself where it had gone so wrong until I noticed that the first thing that happened every month was the reading out of a long list of prayer requests—the first thing that we heard was a long recital of threatening and deadly illnesses, heart attacks, stroke, multiple sclerosis, cancer, Alzheimer's and the rest. These are mighty names and if you have them thrown at you one after the other, as regularly happened at the service, it is almost inevitable that you will sink into sadness and despair under such an onslaught. You can only take on such names when first you have invoked against them the name that is above every name, when you have placed yourself under the power and the protection of the crucified and risen Christ who has taken on all these destructive powers and triumphed over them.

In the church near Belfast where I was minister when the Northern Ireland Troubles were at their worst in the late 1960s and early 1970s, we had a well-attended midweek prayer meeting. In leading it I soon learnt that if you let it start with intercession, it would end in depression. Another bomb attack, another sectarian murder, another wild speech from Ian Paisley—start with all that and you are on a downward slope to the depths of despair. So, we learnt week by week to start with the praise of God, the promises of God, the mighty works of God in the past and the present. When we had focused on these for a while and had tuned in to the hope and joy implicit in them, the point would come when I would say, 'We can start interceding now.' Faithful and fruitful prayer had become possible because we were no longer under the power of the Troubles, but under the good influence of a refreshed relationship to God who has taken on and defeated all our troubles. In the Lord, joy could be anticipated and hope could prevail.

THE PATTERN OF OUR PRAYING

All this has clear implications for the shape of our daily meeting with God. It suggests that we always start with a recollection of and indeed an immersion in his presence and his promises, principally by the reading of scripture supplemented by the liturgical resources our churches offer and our own grateful acknowledgment of God's past generosity towards us in the provision of our needs, the forgiveness of our sins and his specific responses to past prayers. That recognition of the closeness and involvement of God is the gateway to the renewed hope that will allow our expectations to be shaped not primarily by what is happening to us but by what God in his love can be trusted to do for us. Without that grounding in God, our prayers are more likely to be the expressions of, at best, routine ritual and, at worst, hopeless desperation than of the rejoicing in the Lord to which Paul is here calling us. That rejoicing is the gift of the Spirit to those who, before they ask anything, open themselves to God, who is able to give everything.

PRAYER BEGETS GENTLENESS

Paul's next move in our passage is an unexpected one. After he has commended rejoicing in our relationship to God, he goes on to speak of gentleness to other people: 'Let your gentleness be known to everyone' (Philippians 4:5). The connection between the two is not immediately obvious, although the context of the passage helps. Three verses earlier Paul writes: 'I urge Euodia and I urge Syntyche to be of the same mind in the Lord' (v. 2). In other words, there has been a falling-out between two of the leading women in the church. No doubt harsh words have been spoken and negative judgments passed and Paul, who values these women and the contribution they have made to the new Christian community in their city, wants the quarrel between them resolved.

That is why he suggests that those who pray together need to learn how to stay together. In other words, the graciousness of God is catching, and 'gentle graciousness' is a very good translation of the word *epieikes* used here. If we open ourselves up to the gracious God whose generosity towards us makes possible our rejoicing, we shall find it impossible to be harsh towards each other. We shall see that the wrong we think others have done to us is as forgivable as our own wrongdoing and that the bad character we have ascribed to others in our anger with them is open to the transforming grace of God, which is at work in them as surely as it is in us. When Syntyche and Euodia have tuned themselves to the God of the resurrection who buries the past and promises the future, there will be a new forbearance, forgiveness, hope and gentleness in their attitudes to each other, which will open up the possibility of reconciliation between them.

In his plea for gentleness towards others as a result of our exposure in prayer to the graciousness of God, Paul is echoing and applying to his own situation the connection between our relationship with God and our relationship with others made by Jesus in the Lord's Prayer: 'Forgive us our sins as we forgive those who sin against us.' We need to take our bad relationships with others into our prayers with us, so that they may be touched and reshaped by our contact with the gentleness of Jesus and the restoring compassion of God.

PRAYER AND WORRY

From prayer as the begetter of gentleness to others, Paul goes on to prayer as the antidote to worry and fear in ourselves: 'Do not worry about anything, but in everything by prayer and supplication with thanksgiving let your requests be made known to God' (v. 6).

Prayer, and especially intercessory prayer either for ourselves or for others, is not about telling God something that he did not know until we informed him—a point many of those who lead intercessions in church would do well to bear in mind. Rather, we make our requests to God, who is so near to us that he knows what is in our hearts better than we do ourselves, in an act of transferring a burden from our shoulders to his, so that the prime responsibility for what happens rests on him and not on us.

To keep our concerns about people and situations on our own agenda is a recipe for the frustrated anxiety that springs from a realization that we can do so little about them; to pray is to accept God's invitation to put these things on his agenda, confessing that he is the Lord who has resources far beyond ours to deal with what stumps us and who can be trusted to deal with our worries in the mystery and wisdom of the love that he has revealed in Christ. That is why prayer and worry are incompatible opposites: to worry inhibits prayer; to pray at least controls worry.

REQUEST AND RELINQUISHMENT

What we have to make known to God is our requests. To pray is to say to God, 'What I am asking of you is what I see as best for this person or situation, but you are the Lord and, in the very act of asking, I am saying "Over to you." I shall have the first word about what I would like to be done, but you will have the last word and, as I pray, I shall be listening for that word surfacing from the prayer of the Spirit deep within me, and I shall be watching to see how your will is enacted in what actually happens.'

In all intercessory prayer there is a moment of requesting and there is a moment of relinquishment. It is important in prayer not to be too pious too quickly, not to start saying to God what you think he would like to hear but to put the whole thing on a basis of realistic honesty by articulating in your prayer what you are longing for in your heart.

I return yet again to Jesus in Gethsemane. Before he said, 'Your will be done' (Matthew 26:42), he said, 'Father, if it is possible, let this cup pass from me' (v. 39). He was ultimately submissive to the Father, but the concern he submitted was what, at that moment, was pressing hard upon him—his shrinking from the horror before him and his desire to be spared from it: 'I am telling you what my will is but, as I do, I am also telling you that what I want more than my own will is that your will should be done.'

This, I think, is a pattern for how we should pray for someone we care about deeply who is very ill. You start by asking what your love makes you ask for—their recovery—and you urge that on God with all the force of your love. But in the very act of turning the desire into prayer, you submit your desire to God and there will come a moment of relinquishment when you stop urging, when you do not hold on to the sick loved one but hand her over to God, because you know that he has her in his hands and can be trusted with the outcome, whatever it may be.

PERSISTENCE AND SURRENDER

There is a proper persistence in prayer, as the parables of Jesus make clear; we are not easily to take 'no' for an answer. You go on asking until you know that you have been heard. However, there also comes a moment when, by the prompting of the Spirit from the depths of your being, you have to stop asking and start listening, when you have to stop pressing God with your request and instead get ready to receive his answer.

Sometimes I act this out in my own praying: as I pray for a

person, I symbolically hold him in my outstretched hands and then drop my hands as a sign of my faith that I don't need to hold him any longer because he is now being held in the mighty hands of God.

To fail to respond to the moment of relinquishment can mean that a proper persistence degenerates into a stubborn wilfulness. The noise we make with our asking must not drown out the voice of God responding to us. There comes a time of relieved silence when we know that he has heard us and that, in the freedom of his Lordship, he is going to answer us either by doing what we have asked or by doing something else that better accords with the ultimate purposes of his love. It was the latter situation that Jesus had to deal with in Gethsemane and also Paul in his praying about his thorny affliction. That is the moment when, with both of them, we have to say, 'Your will be done.'

THE PROMISE OF PEACE

In the dynamic of our 'I-Thou' relationship with God, explored in these verses from Philippians, we start with God and we end with God. We start on the basis of a joyful confidence in his nearness, which enables us to let our requests be known and, in the end, to relinquish our concerns into his lordly and loving hands.

Paul concludes with a promise: where the intercessory interchange to which we are invited is faithfully undertaken, it will bring us in utterly mysterious ways into a foretaste of that peace, that *shalom* of ultimate well-being, in which the purposes of God are at last perfected for ourselves and for his whole creation. Out of the struggles of our praying, the exaltation of being answered, the desolation of being refused, there comes to us a quiet assurance amid the storms that this is a Father who can be trusted, that this is a Christ whose last word is resurrection, that this is a Holy Spirit who will not leave us until all the purposes of his love for us have been fulfilled. This is the faithful promise to those who pray faithfully: 'The peace of God, which surpasses all understanding, will guard your hearts and your minds in Christ Jesus' (Philippians 4:7).

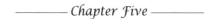

─────── *Chapter Five* ───────

PAUL AND THE PROMISE OF PRAYER

Key Passages: Ephesians 1:15-23; 3:14-20

From Paul's teaching about prayer in Romans and his exhortation to prayer in Philippians, we turn to two examples of Pauline praying in Ephesians. I speak deliberately of 'Pauline praying' rather than 'prayers of Paul' to register my awareness that the authorship of Ephesians is a matter of long and unresolved discussion in New Testament scholarship. For our present purposes, however, it makes little difference whether Paul himself wrote this letter towards the end of his career or whether it is the work of another member of his circle writing in his master's name and under his inspiration, who would therefore have learnt his own praying at Paul's feet. With all that said, I shall go on talking about Paul.

A PRAYER THAT SPRINGS FROM PRAISE

Whoever may be its immediate author, the prayer in Ephesians 1 is thoroughly Pauline in the way it expresses the theology of prayer that we have looked at in Romans and is faithful to the instructions about prayer that we have found in Philippians. The explicit prayer, which starts in Ephesians 1:17, is preceded by a long song of praise at the start of the letter, prefaced by verse 3: 'Blessed be the God and Father of our Lord Jesus Christ, who has blessed us in Christ with every spiritual blessing in the heavenly places' (1:3). Here Paul, faithful to his own exhortation, is indeed rejoicing in the Lord and all that he has done for us in Christ.

From this he goes on to pray in the exalted and expectant recollection of a God who has had us in his purpose and his choice and has predestined us to be his children from before the foundation of the world (vv. 4–5). In Christ and the Spirit he has come near enough to lavish on us the riches of his grace, so that we have redemption and forgiveness to deliver us from the sins of the past in Christ and have our future within his purposes to bring to fulfilment his plan for the renewal and reconciliation of the whole creation (vv. 7–12).

This purpose, formed in the past and to be fulfilled in the future, does not belong to long-gone yesterday or a far distant tomorrow but has begun to work in the present experience of God's people today. In the Holy Spirit, the inheritance that is ours in Christ has started to be delivered in the life and the relationships of God's believing people. This has happened, not just generally wherever the gospel has been proclaimed, but particularly and locally in the church in Ephesus to which this letter is addressed: 'In him [Christ] you also, when you had heard the word of truth, the gospel of your salvation, and had believed in him, were marked with the seal of the promised Holy Spirit' (v. 13).

Paul, as he comes to pray for them, has good reason to give thanks for them because he has heard of their faith in God and their love for one another (vv. 15–16). The lavish generosity of the grace of God who made the world has been rendered effective for our salvation in the living, dying and rising of Jesus and has become a powerful and transforming power in the present through the work of the Holy Spirit. This is a powerful incentive to the prayer that Paul goes on to offer for the church in Ephesus. No wonder that in chapter 3 he has a well-grounded hope that God will not only answer his prayer but also 'by the power at work within us is able to accomplish abundantly far more than all we can ask or imagine' (3:20).

A TRINITARIAN PRAYER

The Lord with whom it starts is the trinitarian God who is at the heart of the theology of prayer we discerned in Romans 8. That is clear from its opening sentence: 'I keep asking that the God of our Lord Jesus Christ, the glorious Father, may give you the Spirit of wisdom and revelation' (1:17, NIV).

Paul is not praying to the shapeless, undefined and featureless deity of a good deal of contemporary radical theology, to say nothing of the folk religion that reflects its vagueness. That kind of God cannot transform our character or our actions because he has no defined character of his own and is so busy affirming everything in general that he never does anything important or particular among us.

In contrast, this prayer is addressed to the God who has given a definitive revelation of himself in his Son, has shown himself to be the Father who has sent the Son and who opens us up to himself in his Spirit. This, in other words, is the prayer of a man who by the Spirit knows *Abba* and by the same Spirit confesses that Jesus is Lord. This prayer is directed to the triune God of the gospel and reflects the promises and the purposes that the gospel reveals.

A PRAYER FOR A LOCAL CHURCH

The distinctive feature of this prayer, which opens up new vistas to us, is that it is a prayer for the Church, not just for the whole Church in general but for the local church in Ephesus to which Paul is writing and to which his readers belong. I got to know the late Cardinal Suenens of Belgium quite well in the later years of his life. One of the unforgettable features of his speaking style at that time was that quite suddenly and without announcement he would stop talking to his audience and start speaking to God. That is what Paul does here; his relationships with God and people are so closely connected that he can move without a break from speaking to Ephesus about God to speaking to God about Ephesus.

Unfortunately, in the contemporary church we often find it difficult to do either. The liturgical speaking about God in the ministry of the word is seldom echoed in the speaking of the congregation over coffee after the service, and the prayers for the church in our liturgical intercessions are seldom carried over as central concerns of the ongoing daily prayers in the lives of its members. That is why liturgy can easily become a marginalized Sunday activity that feels strange and uncomfortable, because what goes on there has little resonance with what takes central place in the rest of our lives. Even people who pray faithfully often find it quite difficult to come to terms with the idea that the local church, its people, its priorities and its needs are to be a central subject of the prayers of its members if it is going to discover and fulfil its mission. Church is the place where you pray for others, but the church itself, in all its joys and sorrows, strengths and weaknesses, does not often enough become a properly focused object of prayer.

We will pray about great international emergencies and national disasters; we will pray, often very faithfully, for individual people who are ill or in the midst of some great personal or family crisis; we might even pray for specific ministers and fellow members in the church as they fulfil their functions within it, but the individualism that has shaped and dominated our culture can make it hard for us to cope with the idea that our church as a corporate entity can accomplish God's purposes only when its corporate life with all its specifics is constantly being opened up to God in the prayers of the people who belong to it.

One of the best-known sayings of Margaret Thatcher, encapsulating so much of the outlook that has shaped us all (whatever we may think of her), was to the effect that there was no such thing as society, only individuals in various degrees of co-operation and competition with one another. Following that through in our present context, there is no such thing as the church, but only an assorted bunch of individuals who are its members and ministers. For these individuals we can and should pray and, in praying for them, we are in effect praying for the church that they comprise.

THE BODY AND ITS MEMBERS

The very word 'members' alerts us to the fact that the New Testament in general and Paul in particular invite us to think of the church in a very different way from that suggested by Margaret Thatcher. In 1 Corinthians, Paul does not talk about individual Christians aggregating into a church but, rather, about a body to which God gives life and energy, which are then distributed among its various members.

It is undoubtedly true that our physical bodies cannot function fully unless all their members—arms, legs, heart, stomach and the rest—are fit enough to make their distinctive contribution to its life and well-being. It is, however, equally true that members severed from the body are lifeless and useless and that each depends for its proper functioning upon what it receives from and gives to the others within the common life of the body.

So, in the church, there is not just a one-way dependence of the body of Christ upon the healthy functioning of all its members in the various gifts and ministries that they bring to it, but an equally significant, though often missed, dependence of the members upon one another within the church, which, as a corporate entity, is much more than the sum of its parts. The members are animated, formed, shaped and renewed by the life of the Spirit, which flows to them through the life they share within the church: 'For just as the body is one and has many members, and all the members of the body, though many, are one body, so it is with Christ' (1 Corinthians 12:12).

OUR CORPORATE IDENTITY

If it is true that the members of a Christian congregation shape the
life of the congregation, it is also true that the corporate life of the
congregation shapes and affects the individual people belonging to
it. Walter Wink[11] has pointed out that the letters from Jesus in the
early chapters of the book of Revelation are addressed to churches
and not to the members of churches, in fact to the 'angel' of the
church at for example Sardis or Philadelphia. He even suggests that
in this context 'angel' means not 'heavenly messenger' but 'corporate identity'.

There were some aspects of the corporate identity of these
churches that furthered the work of Christ among their members and
other aspects that hindered it. In his letters, Jesus commends the one
and rebukes the other. He wants to transform not just the personal
lives of individual church members but the attitudes and the spirit
that prevail and rule the life of the body to which they belong.

I know of two churches, cheek by jowl in the same neighbour-
hood, of the same denomination and very similar churchmanship,
whose members as individuals are very much the same kinds of
people. Yet, the corporate identity of one of these churches is
such that it has fallen out with every minister sent to it, while the
corporate identity of the other is such that it has valued and appreci-
ated the different gifts and contributions of all its leaders. In both
cases the corporate tradition is such a potent factor that it draws the
individual members for good or ill into its influence and under its
powers, so that those who were the critics of the leadership in one
place could as easily have become the admirers in the other.

THE SPIRIT OF THE PLACE

In the same way, when people are asked why they have or have not
joined a particular church, the answers suggest that it was not just
that they had friends who took them there or that the preaching was

good and the worship congenial. Rather, they were attracted or repelled by the whole spirit and feel of the place; by the responsive expectation, or lack of it, that characterized the Sunday services; by the reality, or lack of it, of the way people engaged with God and with one another; whether the church community was, despite its professed welcome, a closed and inward-looking clique of people cosily comfortable with one another and protective of their established ways of doing things, or genuinely open to the people God was sending to it and the challenges their coming might present.

Whether the singing is accompanied by traditional organ or contemporary guitars, and whether the style is formal or informal, the spirit of the place will express itself under and through the outward trappings, and people, discerning it, will be drawn in or put off by it. There are, in fact, churches where the prevailing atmosphere is so dull and deadly that lively Christians will find it hard to stay alive in them, while in other churches the spirit is so vibrant and full of God that dead Christians will have a job not to come alive in them.

DISCERNING THE SPIRITS

All of this suggests important questions that we should be asking about the parishes and congregations to which we belong. How would I describe the corporate identity of the church where I worship? What is there about the spirit of the place that promotes and embodies the gospel and what is there that frustrates and even contradicts it?

The identity of each worshipping community will have been shaped by many different factors: by its past history, by the culture of the wider community in which it is set, by the people who have ministered in it and led it, by its denominational allegiance, by those who openly or more subtly dominate its life at the moment. This corporate identity has been formed by the combination of all these influences, but, when exposed to the gospel, the strengths and weaknesses of that identity will become apparent. In the letters of

Jesus to the first churches, some aspects were to be approved and others needed to be challenged and it will almost certainly be the same with our churches today. The traditions that rule them will have been shaped both by the Spirit of God, who has all the time been at work in them, and by the limitations, prejudices and stubborn self-asserting sinfulness of people who have wanted to have things their own way.

Our future depends on our readiness to discern one from the other and to make the changes required by such discernment. We should not be surprised that the battle between the transforming Spirit and the recalcitrant flesh, which we know on a personal level, is also continuous and can be contentious on a communal level. Churches open to the Spirit will know the ructions that inevitably happen when the power of the Spirit challenges the power of the status quo and of those who have invested in it.

A TRINITARIAN EVALUATION

It can be useful to pursue this process of self-evaluation in trinitarian terms. We can ask if we are perhaps a church that wants to relate primarily to God the Father and therefore sits rather loosely to the gospel of the Son. Father-orientated churches will be more aware of God's transcendence than of his nearness, will find it harder to trust revealed truth and will be more aware of impenetrable mystery. 'Father' churches tend to be suspicious and critical of the claimed certainties of others and accommodating rather than challenging towards the prevailing attitudes of the cultures to which they belong. The 'Father' such churches are left with is often, in his distance and inactivity, quite unlike the loving *Abba* who, in his transforming love, makes himself known only in and through Jesus his Son.

We can also ask ourselves if perhaps we belong to a Jesus-orientated church, concentrating on a personal relationship with a personal saviour and the individualistic religion to which this can lead. Such churches can forget that the God of the gospel is not just the private saviour of souls but the creator and redeemer of the world and that his will is to be done and his kingdom is to come to every part of this world. He is a God who will winkle us out from the isolation of our piety and make us witnesses to his truth and love in the ordinary workaday life of the world and the great issues it presents to us. We should remember that 'God so loved *the world...*' (John 3:16).

An alternative, quite probable in the contemporary context, is that we might find we have become a Spirit-orientated church, concentrating on dramatic experiences of spiritual renewal and the exercise of supernatural charismatic gifts, more concerned with testimonies of what has been happening to us than with the good news of what God has done for us in Christ. Such churches, in the midst of such heady and thrilling experiences, are liable to forget that the defining work of the Holy Spirit is not to inspire tongues and prophecies, healings and swoonings but rather to lead us to confess God as *Abba* and Jesus as Lord.

In the mercy of God, churches are not abandoned to the three kinds of one-sidedness that we have been outlining. Father, Son and Holy Spirit are so intimately united and connected that, even if you are tempted to concentrate on your relationship with one of them, he will lead you to relate appropriately to the others as well. One of the ways in which he will do that is precisely by exposing our church life as it is to the judgment and correction of the gospel of the triune God, so that we can detect where we have got out of kilter with the gospel and what needs to be done to bring us back into the fullness of our relationship with the triune God, who is always and equally the Father above us, the Son with us and the Spirit among us.

Such a trinitarian audit of the life of the local church sets the context for Paul's prayer for the local church in Ephesus. He prays that he 'may give you the Spirit of wisdom and revelation, so that you may know him better' (Ephesians 1:17, NIV). He is, in effect, asking that the Ephesians should be given a realistic understanding of both God and the church to which they belong, so that they may be able to discover whether and how far it is the Holy Spirit who presides over and shapes that church's life.

UNHOLY SPIRITS

All sorts of very unholy spirits can, in fact, preside over and shape the life of our churches and can do so stealthily, almost without our noticing, so that we become blind to what is controlling us. In these circumstances, we do indeed need the Spirit of wisdom and revelation to let us know God better so that in his light we can also know ourselves better and see where the Holy Spirit's purposes are being hindered and frustrated.

The unholy spirits are easier to name in general than to identify in particular. We can deplore their influence in the abstract and succumb to them in the specific; we can spot what is wrong in other Christian communities and be oblivious to the same defects among ourselves. On the one hand, there is the spirit of conservatism, which hangs on for dear life to the status quo and is so busy claiming how effective and productive it was in the last generation that those under its sway easily fail to see how ineffective and obstructive it has now become. On the other hand, there is the spirit of restlessness that is impatient with everything traditional and wants to cut the church off from all that was good in its past— throw out the organ and bring in the guitars, abandon the liturgy and bring in the charismatic gifts, abandon the reflective silences in which the word can do its work for the relentless noisiness, every minute filled with singing. Such obsession with our activity can drive out dependence on God's grace.

Often these two attitudes—conservatism and restlessness—are fighting with each other in our churches, and it can take a great deal of discernment in the Spirit to sort out what in each of them is positively receptive and negatively resistant to the gospel. Both reverent formality and spontaneous informality can be useful to the

Spirit but can also dull our ears to his voice.

There are also many churches in our own day, especially perhaps in affluent suburbia, where the Spirit of holiness is inhibited by a spirit of unholy complacency in which we filter out from the scriptural gospel all that could challenge and change us and replace it with an idea that God's love is affirmative of all we are and do. We offer an undisturbing, easygoing gospel that has lost its awareness of God's judgment, which rejects everything in our lives that defies and contradicts his love and calls us to be transformed into a more credible reflection of the divine holiness into which the Spirit seeks to change us.

If, in the past, church discipline was harsh, judgmental and overly concerned with the sins of the flesh, nowadays it is almost absent and highly questionable relationships are tolerated and condoned without any exercise of a pastoral discipline that would call people to repentance and guide them to lifestyles more worthy of the gospel they profess.

Along with the spirit of idolatry that makes us cherish a building or a form of churchmanship more than we cherish the living God, there are various spirits of domination in which one group subjugates the whole life of a church to its sway. Even today, there is the domination of the ordained minister who, instead of being content to conduct the orchestra, as it were, sets himself up as the one-man-band who plays all the instruments. Equally common is the domination of some specialized group within the congregation, often the musicians, whether in the traditional form of organist or choir or the modern worship leaders with music groups. Small churches can easily be controlled by wealthy members who make large contributions and expect to have their own way, and all churches are liable to be subjected to the idiosyncratic agendas of strong personalities, whose influence persists long after they themselves have gone. All these people or groups aggressively or, more often, subtly shade the windows and bar the doors so that God's good light and healthy fresh air cannot get through.

These spirits can take over uninvited and sometimes nearly un-noticed until some conflict or crisis jolts us into awareness of what has been ruling the roost for a very long time among us. Often such conflicts and crises are the opportunities that the Holy Spirit can use to show us the defects that he wants to remedy, the imbalances he wants to correct and the deficiencies he wants to supply, so that we can be left wondering if such conflicts are not part of his deliberate strategy to wake us up to his way and his will for us.

INVOKING THE HOLY SPIRIT

What is distinctive about the Holy Spirit when set against all these other dominating influences that shape our churches is that, while they are there uninvited, the Holy Spirit comes only where he is asked. We are reminded again of Luke's version of the promise of Jesus: 'Your heavenly Father goes on being willing to go on giving the Holy Spirit to those who go on asking him' (Luke 11:13, author's translation). That is why specific, continuing prayer for the coming of the Holy Spirit into the particular situations and crises of our parish is of such paramount importance. That is why, in our passage, Paul prays just such a prayer for the church in Ephesus, and this prayer needs to be echoed in our own churches.

The other spirits invade and can hold churches captive, but the Holy Spirit comes where he is wanted, sought and faithfully prayed for—sometimes by a small group of people who have seen that what their church needs is something only God can supply and have committed themselves to asking on behalf of others (and sometimes without the knowledge of their fellow members) that God should give them what they need. When times of renewal have come to churches, it has often been discovered that years before a few people have been seeking just such a renewal from God without knowing how or when it would come. That is why we need to ask if, by whom and with what degree of priority prayer for the Spirit is being offered in the churches to which we belong.

MANY COMINGS: ONE SPIRIT

Notice that Paul does not pray for the coming of the Holy Spirit as if he had been absent until this point. His prayer is not for people who are potential converts, that they should know the Holy Spirit for the first time, but for committed Christians, that they should know him better. Paul prays for the Spirit, who was in fact the agent of their conversion in the past and who has been at work among them ever since, that he would come upon them in a new way for a new day. They are not to go on living out of the experiences of the past but are to be revitalized in the present and for the future in a way that is both faithful to the given gospel and relevant to the contemporary situation and its specific opportunities and needs.

The Gospel stories contain not just one definitive coming of the Holy Spirit, but different comings that build on one another. That is true of both the life of Jesus and the life of the church. It is by the coming of the Holy Spirit that Jesus is first conceived and made flesh in the womb of Mary, and it is by a new coming of the Holy Spirit in his Jordan baptism that he is anointed for his messianic ministry with its requirement of new power and fresh gifts. In the case of the disciples, there is the quiet breathing of the Spirit upon them by the risen Jesus on Easter evening, as recorded by John, as well as the dramatic descent of the Spirit on the nascent Christian community on the day of Pentecost to empower it for its mission first to the Jewish and then to the Gentile world.

In other words, the coming of the Spirit is always appropriate to the people to whom he comes and their needs and ministry in their current situation, which may be quite different now from what it was ten years ago. Yesterday's blessing will not be adequate to today's demands and the fact that we need a new empowering by the same Spirit does not in any way deny the reality of what he has done in the past but seeks the same power, which operated in one way then, to operate in a new way now. The basic business of the

Spirit is to communicate to us the full riches that have come to us in Christ, and these riches are far too great to be given in a single experience at one given moment but have to be sought afresh in all their variety. When we remember that, it is entirely appropriate for Paul to pray for the Ephesians, who already know the Spirit, to come to know him better.

Looking back on my own experience, I am aware of the diverse ways in which the one Spirit has worked in me at different stages of my life. All the way through he has been the Spirit of faith, who has enabled me to know God as Abba and Jesus as Lord, not in my case in a memorable moment of conversion but in a long process of realizing and maturing the relationship with the triune God into which I was baptized. In my young adulthood he was to me the Spirit of my vocation by whom I was very clearly and decisively called away from all the other career possibilities that beckoned me and into the ordained ministry of the Word and sacraments, which has filled my years and my days. In my middle life he came again, this time as the Spirit of charismatic renewal who drew me from the abstractions of theological thinking into participation in the eventfulness of the God who can transform our relationships with himself and with others and can give us a taste of victory in our inward struggles with our own residual unredeemed nature. Now in my old age, when I have to prepare to part company one by one with the things and people that have been my joys and my supports, he is the Spirit who draws me further and further into dependence on the faithful and living God. That deep dependence is the key to the future and to the fulfilment in the new creation of the work and the relationships that have been central to life here. As Paul put it, in a not altogether different context: 'Now there are varieties of gifts, but the same Spirit; and there are varieties of services, but the same Lord; and there are varieties of activities, but it is the same God who activates all of them in everyone' (1 Corinthians 12:4).

A SPIRITUAL AUDIT

Making a spiritual audit of our own churches, the negative side is to recognize our deficiencies and failings, but the positive side is to open ourselves up in prayer to the Spirit so that we can receive the new thing he wants to do in us now, which will continue and complement what he has done in the past. The shadow side of past blessings is that they can harden into fixed traditions, closing us up to new blessings to come.

Last summer, a child let go of the string of the helium balloon she was carrying home outside our front window. The balloon was carried upwards but got entrapped in the telephone wires above the street, where the gas seeped away and left us with a piece of inert coloured plastic stuck in the wires, which became more and more ragged and decayed. This is a parable of what can happen in churches. Once we were full of the Spirit, raising us towards the skies; without the Spirit we could not have got where we are, but the Spirit has seeped out and we are left stuck and decaying in the imprisoning wires of tradition.

All the humanly devised programmes, initiatives and managerial readjustments cannot get us airborne again—only a fresh filling of the same Spirit with which we started can do that. The programmes, along with new forms of ministry and well-judged enterprises of mission, all have their place, but they will come to nothing unless they are animated by the Spirit of God, who is the Lord and giver of life to the church. This Spirit comes where the church is opened up to him by the intercessions, private and corporate, of those members who pray for their churches the same prayer that Paul prayed for Ephesus: 'I pray that the God of our Lord Jesus Christ, the Father of glory, may give you a spirit of wisdom and revelation as you come to know him' (Ephesians 1:17).

WHAT THE SPIRIT BRINGS

Paul's prayer does not stop at this point but goes on to enumerate and to pray for some of the ways in which the Spirit will manifest his presence in our churches as he undertakes whatever specific changes to our corporate identity and common life he sees are appropriate to the stage we have reached and the mission we have to fulfil: 'I pray… that, with the eyes of your heart enlightened, you may know what is the hope to which he has called you, what are the riches of his glorious inheritance among the saints, and what is the immeasurable greatness of his power for us who believe' (vv. 17–19).

The evidence that the Spirit has begun to have his way in any church, and therefore the evidence for which we have to pray in our own churches, is here summed up as hope, riches and power. These words remind us that the Spirit will always act to create an atmosphere of hope, plenty and effectiveness. In all his doings he is the Spirit of expectation, of enthusiastic energy and of active eventfulness.[12]

THE SPIRIT OF HOPE

A Scottish Presbyterian minister, presumably in one of those low, despairing moments that can afflict us all, once described his congregation as 'an anaemic bunch of peely-wally no-hopers', which graphically sums up the feel of churches in which the Holy Spirit is in short supply. In the churches of the Western world there are of course lots of temptations to that kind of despair—after a century of numerical decline in a culture where indifference to the gospel shows signs of turning into hostility towards it, it is not surprising that the people of God should see themselves as a beleaguered and ageing minority whose hopes do not extend far beyond their own short-term survival, with all the debilitating spiritual consequences that entails for the life of the fellowship. The only possibility of escape from such a situation is a repentant turning round, away from the survey of discouraging trends around us and to a fresh engagement with the gospel that has the risen Jesus as its centre. When Mary Magdalene looked at the empty tomb where all her hopes were lost, she wept, but when she turned round and, at his word, recognized the risen Jesus, her expectations became boundless and her extinguished hopes were reborn.

In dark moments of the church's life, the risen Jesus calls us to turn round again to his risen presence, which in practice means to open ourselves in prayer to the springs of life at the heart of our gospel until we come into revitalizing contact with the great 'But God' of Easter morning. This is the God who, at the moment when things are at their most hopeless, can act decisively to reverse the trend and, at the very moment when all seems lost, can stage a resurrection.

The burial of the body of Christ, the Church, has often been foretold—in glee by his enemies and sometimes in tears by his friends. But no undertaker has ever had his fee for that funeral: funny things are liable to happen on the morning of the third day. So it has proved again and again in the long history of the Church. When we, by our sin and unbelief, have made a sorry mess of things and see no way to set them to rights, God comes good on his covenant and his promises and, by his grace, the body of Christ rises from the dead. This gives birth to the hope, 'Tomorrow is also God's!' When the sun goes down on the bleak present, the last word has not been spoken, because God's tomorrow is still to come, and the Spirit, when he is prayed for, can take the objective and historical hope anchored in the resurrection of Jesus and make it the basis of a new and vibrant expectation in the life of local churches. As we pray, we come to see that the possibilities are not limited by the statistical trends produced by computerized despair but by the sovereign interventions of God who loves us, who comes where he is invited and can be expected to do something incalculably different from anything we either plan or dread.

These hopes and expectations do not remain entirely in a future that never arrives but become part of the present experience of a praying church. That is what Paul means when he speaks of knowing 'what are the riches of his glorious inheritance among the saints, and what is the immeasurable greatness of his power to us who believe' (v. 19). Prayer is sustained by the fact that things happen, which we can recognize as God's response to our asking.

The mystery of 'now' and 'not yet'

This does not happen always and everywhere, but it does happen sometimes and somewhere and, when it does, it is an encouraging sign, foretaste and promise of what God can do for us and among us. Paul says in verse 14 of this chapter that we have received the Holy Spirit as 'a pledge of our inheritance'. The Greek word here is *arrabon*, which means a down payment or a first instalment promising that the rest, which we do not yet have, is on its way. What happens now is glorious and wonderful because it shows us that God is at work on our behalf in ways we could ourselves neither contrive nor expect. Nevertheless, not everything God has promised happens here and now; much is reserved for the small tomorrow of our earthly future or for the great Tomorrow of God's completed kingdom.

Why all our prayers are not answered, including the ones clearly based on God's promise and purpose, why all the sick are not healed, all relationships not mended, all our besetting sins not rooted out, why a good thing happens to one person and not to another who seems to need it more is the mystery we encounter in prayer. These are all insoluble questions that have no answer except for the faith that God knows what he is doing and will do it in accordance with his own timetable and not ours.

EVENTFULNESS NOW

Trust for what does not happen is sustained and nourished by our joyful wonder at what does happen in the present. Again and again

God does act: prayers are answered; an unlikely Saul of Tarsus is converted into Paul the apostle; somebody who was ill gets better in defiance of the best medical prognosis; churches that were in their death-throes are brought to life and are used to draw people to the gospel and to show the love of Christ in the world to which they belong. The power of the Spirit is ultimately unlimited, but when and where he acts belongs to the mystery of his sovereignty. But when his power falls, things happen that are wonderful in our eyes.

The eventfulness accompanying God's prayed-for presence is the preliminary vindication of the hope inspired in us by the Spirit. When our prayer opens the door to a new coming of the Holy Spirit, the gospel moves out from the realm of fine talk and unfulfilled promise into the realm of divine action. This action bears witness to the fact that God lives and Christ is risen and is doing things now that are pledges and promises of even greater things still to come. When that happens, the church stops being a tired and boring place and becomes not a perfect place where the rule of God holds sway in all its fullness, but a credible place where again and again events happen as a result of its praying, which proclaim that there is a God who is reached by prayer and responds to it in his Spirit.

This is, in fact, what Jesus said would occur when people were open to the Spirit that the Father would send: 'The one who believes in me will also do the works that I do and, in fact, will do greater works than these, because I am going to the Father' (John 14:12). To see the works of Jesus done among us is the rich inherit-ance of the saints (Ephesians 1:18) pledged and delivered to us by the Holy Spirit (v. 14). This picks up one of the central verses in Romans 8 that we looked at earlier, where Paul tells us that we are heirs of God and joint heirs of Christ (see Romans 8:17).

One of the great services that the charismatic renewal rendered to all the churches in the second half of the 20th century is the expectation that we should see the works of God being done, not just in the New Testament past or the heavenly future, but here and now, where we are. This was accompanied by a rediscovery and reclamation of the charismatic gifts, such as prophecy, healing and often speaking in tongues. These gifts, rightly used, are indeed tools in the hand of the Spirit; but they always need to be considered in the wider context of the whole thrust of the Spirit's work. The rule of God, which began to give signs of its presence in the ministry of Jesus, should continue to give the same signs in the ministry of the people among whom Christ lives and works.

WORLDWIDE SIGNS OF RESURRECTION

What Jesus did in the microcosm of Galilee and Jerusalem has gone on being done in the macrocosm of the worldwide body of Christ all over the world, across the continents and down the centuries in an endless array of cultural contexts. Disciples are called, sinners are forgiven, the sick are healed, apostles are sent and communities are created that, within and beyond themselves, witness to the universal love of God in their concern and work for the right sharing of resources and the just ordering of relationships in the whole human society that God seeks to claim for his love. All this requires long and unrelenting human effort, but that effort needs to be supported by the Spirit, who inspires and sustains the effort, who alone can change the inner hearts of people and the corporate identity of our churches and communities. This is indeed work for the Spirit and the Spirit comes where he is prayed for.

Paul's context is cosmic, but his focus is local. His Christ is seated in the heavenly places as Lord over all, but the place where his resurrection power for the world is released is among the local Christians in Ephesus and local churches like them. The power of the Spirit that he prays for for Ephesus is the very same power that raised Christ from the dead and seated him over all things at the right hand of God.

THE PROMISE OF PRAYER

In Christian prayer as Paul shows it to us, we are involved with the very life of the triune God. We pray to the Father by sharing in the intercession of the Son that is echoed in us by the intercession of the Spirit. In prayer, we move from the submission of our whole lives to God as Jesus did in Gethsemane to expectation of the outpouring of the Spirit who worked resurrection in Jesus and who will work the same in us as a foretaste and promise of what he will ultimately do in all the world. It is in this presence and this promise that we are called to pray in Jesus' name.

In recognition of all this we can, perhaps with a renewed and awestruck understanding and a fresh commitment, pray with Paul for ourselves and our churches what he once prayed for his:

For this reason I bow my knees before the Father, from whom every family in heaven and on earth takes its name. I pray that, according to the riches of his glory, he may grant that you may be strengthened in your inner being with power through his Spirit, and that Christ may dwell in your hearts through faith, as you are being rooted and grounded in love. I pray that you may have the power to comprehend, with all the saints, what is the breadth and length and height and depth, and know the love of Christ that surpasses knowledge, so that you may be filled with all the fullness of God. Now to him who by the power at work within us is able to accomplish abundantly far more than we can ask or imagine, to him be glory in the church and in Christ Jesus to all generations, forever and ever. Amen.
EPHESIANS 3:14–21

✣

NOTES

1 Paul Tillich, *The Shaking of the Foundations*, Pelican, 1962, pp. 46–58

2 John Robinson, *Honest to God*, SCM Press, 1963

3 Lawrence Freeman, *The Tablet*, Volume 260, no. 8622, 14 January 2006, p. 13

4 'Crown Him with Many Crowns', Matthew Bridges (1890–94) and Godfrey Thring (1823–1903)

5 Gordon D. Fee, *God's Empowering Presence*, Paternoster, 1995, p. 517

6 Doctrine Commission of the Church of England, *We Believe in God*, Church House Publishing, 1994

7 *We Believe in God*, p. 108

8 Gordon Fee, *God's Empowering Presence*, Paternoster, 1995

9 André Louf, *Teach us to Pray*, Darton, Longman & Todd, 1991, p. 18

10 Heribert Mühlen, *Der Heilige Geist in Person*. This has not been translated into English but is discussed in Tom Smail's book *Giving Gift*, Darton, Longman & Todd, 1994, p. 154.

11 Walter Wink, *Naming the Powers*, Marshall Pickering, 1988, p 108, compare p. 104

12 Eventfulness: this word is used to convey the idea that the Holy Spirit is at work in the observable world of outward events and not just in the inner world of subjective experience.